Seven Years of Love

For the Woman Who Desires to Love Well

Katrina McCain
www.KatrinaMcCain.com

Seven Years of Love by Katrina McCain
Published 2020
United States of America

Permission has been obtained for usage of all personal accounts.

Images taken by Monisa J. Photography
https://monisajphotography.com

For Jarrett,
I loved you before I met you.
At the end of our lives, when they speak of our love, my
forever prayer is that they remember that you loved me well.

*"Above all, be loving.
This ties everything together perfectly."*
~Colossians 3:14

CONTENTS

From One Wife to Another

I think it's safe to say that all of us desire genuine and fulfilling love. Maybe you're enjoying the bliss of being a newlywed, or maybe you have come across some bumps in the road. Either way, I know you desire to keep loving in your marriage. I share that, as well! This is why I wrote this book. It's my way of reaching far out to you, across the states, maybe even across the seas, to tell you that no matter the seasons you will eventually find yourself in, loving well is possible – in spite of our circumstances, feelings, fears or mistakes.

I want you to know upfront that I am writing to you from my heart – from one wife to another. Consider this book to be our personal conversation over lunch or over a cup of coffee. I don't know you, but I truly care about you and I care about your marriage and I want you to trust me when I tell you that your desire to love well doesn't go unseen by the Lord. Your joys aren't accidental and your tears are not in vain. Everyone's marriage is different, but cultivating a good marriage has more to do with the living than with the feelings. If there is love, then your marriage is alive and capable of thriving and becoming all that God has purposed for you. With that being said, I want to focus this book on encouraging you to continue making strives to love well and to be loved well, regardless of the distractions around you.

Though this book is about marriage, even if you're single and hoping to be married, I applaud you for flipping through these pages! I pray treasures will be stored in your heart to better equip you for your future marriage should that be God's plan for you! For those of you who are currently married, I pray this book will encourage and remind you that the Gospel of Christ is applicable for every season, every heart and every marriage. His eternal love never fails and it's this love that will propel us to love well. Even when it's hard, our marriages can still produce great joy. We can live lives of love, have amazing sex with our misters and build a confidence to love like Jesus, though it may cost us our comfort zones.

This book is for any woman who desires to love beyond her feelings and above the inconsistent deceptions of this culture. I pray this time we share together will motivate you to continue to lure your husband with a gentle spirit, erect his trust in your virtue, blaze your heart with prayer and love confidently and courageously with the power of God's unfailing love!

I hope you're excited! I'll see you in Chapter One!

In Christ's Love,

<u>CHAPTER 1</u>

BUILDING BETTER LOVE

Jarrett makes me smile. Just say his name at random and watch me light up! I'm serious. It's silly really, but I can honestly say that I am whimsically and full heartedly in love with my man! We've been through a lot together, though in the grand scheme of life, we're still in the beginning. It's all been a blessing, but the glow I carry is not because we've had a perfect marital experience. We've certainly had our rainy days. Early on, though, I thought that Jarrett McCain was the most wonderful person on the planet - I still do! He was (and is) insightful, truthful, strong and immensely affectionate. But, when I look over our three years of dating and seven years of marriage, I've had to give grace over the reality that he isn't perfect, and neither am I. Wonderful? Yes! Perfect? No.

Since the day we exchanged our vows, we've had our fair share of disagreements, life challenging chaos, misdirection, stubborn pride and other whirlwinds at random. Loving isn't always lovely and though my heart yearns for the ease of constant romance, what I am discovering is that building better love involves gaining the vital maturity that challenges ultimately produce.

As we all soon come to realize, it takes more than cake and kisses to sustain a fulfilling love and in the depths of my heart, I know you are a woman who is open to all the glorious seasons that await for you in your marriage! Seven years of loving and growing with someone has been quite a blessing to me and I don't take any of this for granted. I still smile because the seasons of challenges that my marriage has endured, including those yet to come, haven't been given permission to penetrate our love. Marriage is work, as we all will discover, and though we pray for the best, we are often caught off guard by the tests. I want to encourage you that your trials are not your enemy; they are your teacher and your trainer. They are uncomfortable, but they are the weight in which to strengthen your marriage and produce unique formation within the story of your love. The misunderstandings and conflicts will come and will sometimes find their way to intertwine between the tapestry of your joys, your celebrations and your dreams, however it's the abstracts of the unexpected that design unique loveliness.

I believe we all yearn for a sense that we are completely and fully known and fully loved and fully understood and accepted without question. It's a deep and aching craving within our hearts because we were created for perfection and our souls cry out for it. In the beginning of time, we were perfect beings, living in a perfect world with perfect bodies and perfect lives, but one day that changed (see Genesis chapter 2). Once imperfection came into this world, our surroundings fell under the burden of sin, but the craving of our souls still cries out for our lost perfection. It's why we feel frustrated when things don't go as planned. It's why we experience resentment when our husbands don't respond in the way we expect. Perfection is something we all wrestle with from time to time, but I'm here to tell you that building better love has nothing to do with perfect pictures – those in our heads or those on our screens.

I know that many of us willingly walked into marriage believing that it would realize a piece of perfection for us. We thought marriage would end our search for acceptance, belonging and understanding – that a relationship would consummate our personal worth and fill our empty spaces. I've spoken with many women from different walks of life who have been stunned by the reality that, though they love their husbands, they did not marry a perfect person and that their lives did not turn out to be the picture-perfect reality they thought marriage would create. What was in their heads did not manifest within their homes. I'm no different.

On June 1, 2013, I took Jarrett's last name with full expectancy that the bad times wouldn't be that bad and that our love was strong enough to move past every pain and bolster through all the problems … maybe even prevent them. It was naïve, but this was my sincere perspective on the matter. I grew up in a beautiful Christian home with parents who were devoted to each other and to the Lord. I saw their kisses and overheard their apologies and prayers. I saw my Father envelope my Mother into his arms on a daily basis. I also heard the clamor of my Mother fussing and arguing, only to watch her passionately and romantically swoon over the same man for 37 years. I've seen my Dad storm out into the back yard in efforts to recharge from kitchen quarrels over private school bills and differences of opinion, only to quickly turn around and take my mother's hand and glide her around our home in a private dance for my brother and I to enjoy. This was my childhood. This was my first and greatest example of loving well. Yes, I saw their challenges, but I also saw their loving.

I knew marriage involved both, but I didn't realize the weight that loving well tends to demand. I was quite inexperienced in the sacrifice required in loving well, as the majority of newly married people are. Most of us are realist and expect a few bumps in the road of life, but none of us are immune to the unpredictable occurrences and consequences that come with uniting ourselves to another human being. I may have had a front seat witness to the beauty and strength of my parents' marriage, but I had yet to experience the process of loving well, firsthand. What a difference there is between seeing love and living it out. It's in the living where the challenges occur, but there is always hope that the love which created our marriages will take us through. It begins first with knowing the unfailing love of Jesus through the gift of the Gospel. Experiencing His love propels our own.

We cannot strategically avoid what life determines. Though we have our plans, God direct our paths (Proverbs 16:9). Sometimes, those paths take us through challenges that are meant to prepare us for greater capacities to appreciate the love we've been given. This is the grace of God: that He turns all things into good for anyone who puts their trust and love in Him (Romans 8:28). Because of this truth, the circumstances in your life that are sure to surround your marriage have no control over the mission, purpose or identity Christ is cultivating within your union.

Love won't prevent the problems, but it can prevail through them as we seek the Lord's love and apply it in our marriages. This is what takes us from good to great; from existing in our marriages and into experiencing a flourishing unity into living and loving on mission and into purpose. There are insurmountable joys to look forward to, but loving well isn't limited to circumstantial thrills. We don't have to live for the weekend in our marriages. We can live and love greatly throughout our lives, come what may. So, what if I told you that enjoying your marriage has nothing to do with pleasure? What if I told you that becoming a wife who loves well is possible in the joyful and the challenging seasons that are sure to invade your lives?

Ladies, life is full of messes, but even in it lies abundant blessings! Throwing away the picture-perfect idea that marriage should always be pretty, tidy and shiny has given me so much freedom! None of us are perfect, therefore our marriages won't be perfect, either. Let those expectations fade away, because a good marriage has absolutely nothing to do with perfection.

A Lovely Tool

Marriage can become a lovely tool used to mold us into living better and loving better when the perfect love of God becomes a part of our story. He has a purpose for your marriage, and I promise you that it has nothing to do with what you originally thought. This is why I love Proverbs 16: 33 so much.

"You can roll the dice, but the Lord determines how they fall." (NLT)

The Lord's plans for your marriage are deeper and fuller than you could even imagine, and He desires to order your steps and guide you into His will for your heart and for your home. It's important that we cling to this truth, because in marriage, we're going to have moments when we just aren't sure. We're going to face aspects of life that we didn't plan for or expect. We will experience characteristics and habits in our husbands that we didn't see while we were dating them. The same is true for us. We will see sides of ourselves that we were unaware of until marriage, but all this leads us to loving better, because it's through these unknowns that God's hand brings about His plans.

On our own, our best attempts fall so short of God's glorious abundance which is ours through Jesus (Ephesians 3: 20-21). It's easy to overlook, but it's impossible to deny and as women who desire to love well, we must remember that we have been given the power to love in the moments that aren't perfect, by leaning into the unfailing love of Christ, which is perfect. He has promised to complete a good work in us (Philippians 1:6) and He is using every aspect of our lives, including our marriages, to bring about this good completion.

Marriage will never be what we thought it was supposed to be, but it can develop into what it is purposed to be. God is in control and He desires to use your marriage to transform your heart into a woman who becomes an ambassador of His unfailing love not only in your home, but also in this world!

<u>The Difference in Dating</u>

Jarrett took me to Ben and Jerry's on our first date. It was a pretty day in May, a Wednesday evening, right before church. I couldn't stop talking because I was so nervous! He hardly said a word. He just had this half-moon smile on his face as he listened to me go on and on about school and modeling, traveling, horse riding and my family. I remember the ice cream started melting and dripping on my fingers – a sign to stop talking and eat! It was a lovely moment that would lead to dozens of other lovely moments, but what I find so tender is the fact that, though we had such a nice time, there was messy ice cream on my hands.

Loving well will involve messes, mistakes and mess ups. The charge to us all, however, is to live passed the feelings and passed the predictabilities and comforts that our control tries to cling to. Marriage is completely different than your dating relationships and therefore, requires alternative means to be governed by. In dating, there are a lot of predictable patterns, ultimatums and equal exchanges. But marriage isn't 50/50. Instead, two people learn to deny themselves for the other in ways that neither thought was possible or required. There must be grace for the messes and hope for the renewing of mercies for one another in each passing day.

Though a dating relationship can lead us to marriage, it can never prepare us for marriage. To be completely honest, marriage is not an extension of dating at all; it is its own and unique entity and it requires values and virtues that dating doesn't entail. In dating, you get to learn the other person; in marriage, you get to learn how to love the other person in ways that will change both of your lives forever.

At the core of who I am, I desire to encourage you and to share the beautiful truth of Christ's love with you. Some of what will be discussed in the next chapters will conflict with trending relationship practices society hails. Some topics I will share will lift you and some of it will challenge you, but all of it is written to celebrate you, your marriage and your life. Dating is a wonderful thing, but marriage supersedes it and therefore requires more grace, greater intentionality and the presence of the perfect love of Christ. It's His love that covers all error (1 Peter 4:8). It's His grace that leads us into His promises. Dating is lovely, but it's not synonymous with marriage. There are many differences between the two, the main one being is that marriage is a commitment not just to each other but also to God. This commitment and mutual focus drives a marriage beyond self-interests and into the spiritual challenge and mission of submission to something beyond ourselves. Often times in dating, challenges and conflicts can push us apart, but in marriage, they can bond us together when our mutual focus is on pleasing God in the ways in which we choose to love each other. Of course, we all have aspirations for our relationships to be smooth, uncomplicated and enjoyable, but let's not overlook the importance of trials and how they can produce patience, endurance and transformation (Romans 5:4).

The reality is that though marriage is beautiful, it is also very challenging and sadly, many people aren't intentionally and purposefully preparing for marriage in their dating relationships. Many marriages occur as a "next step"; the assumption being that marriage will make life better, more beautiful, more complete. Dating often focuses on fun and sex and compatibility, but not marriage; not really. This is because our culture centers itself around the false assumption that good feelings and fun experiences in dating will produce an effortless love for decades to come. But this just isn't true. See, in dating, we are more lenient, more apt to overlook shortcomings and inconsistencies. It's not faking, but more like an exaggeration of perspective concerning the person we are involved with. This has a lot to do with our tolerant levels, past experiences and our stages in life; it's also very influenced by our hormones. These frilly little feelings are often confused for love and they motivate us to present our best selves in a dating relationship because we want to earn the returned feelings from the person we've been captivated by. This sort of exchange isn't unconditional love; it's performance based and it needs to be fed often.

Performance based love demands to be catered to and becomes disgruntled when feelings fade. But no feelings, no matter how good, will last forever. Eventually, even in marriage, the sensations of those "in-love" hormones quiet down and take a back seat as the reality of life sojourns us on into careers, parenthood and other various seasons of life. Romance is lovely, but it's not constant. We can make a priority to be romantic and this is important, but if our love is contingent on romance and the thrills of sex and passion, we've got some reevaluating to do.

According to science, our bodies secret an emotional love hormone called oxytocin. These physical sensations last for about two years.[1] Eventually, either due to time or circumstances, it begins to decline. This doesn't necessarily mean that your body is no longer producing the chemical, but its sensations aren't felt in the same intense ways as they did during dating or newlywed years. I'm sure you're not surprised to know that once these feelings abate, many relationships begin to lose heart, lose focus and lose affection. That's because the feelings (or the absence of feelings) do not insure lasting love.

There are so many reasons and factors as to why people choose to marry one another, but marriage is not going to Big-Bang eternal happiness into your life. The good feelings will fade. The

---

[1] Ahmora, Devou. *How Science Guides Our Love Lives*. Althea Press, 2010.

tingles and the butterflies will eventually dissolve, and compatibility will seem questionable at times. Every now and then, they come back, but then they will leave again because feelings cannot carry our hope. The life you've chosen with your husband won't always feel good and honestly, it wasn't meant to. What marriage was truly meant for goes further than feelings could every carry you. It's something that dating can never prepare you for, but something that loving well can produce within your lives, forever.

A Good Marriage

Loving well requires an appreciation for what is true and this will produce a confidence in us all to admit that we are flawed people – not excusing our flaws, but admitting that they are there and dealing with them, rather than brushing them to the side in attempts to move on or to avoid what we do not wish to admit to ourselves or to others. Honesty is powerful and it cultivates transparency. It's this vulnerability that provides our lives with opportunities to love well and to be loved well. It starts with us first (Matthew 7:3). We must always start with ourselves because truth and vulnerability begins when we look into our own eyes, instead of trying to remove the specks in other people's (Matthew 7:5).

I know, I know … I don't know your husband like you do. I don't know what you've been through. I don't know what he's done or didn't do. I don't know his inconsistencies or bad habits or the years of conflict that you've had to endure throughout your relationship. I know, I know … none of this seems to apply to you. You're in love and everything is going great in your marriage. You have no complaints or concerns right now. Your sex is good, your vibe is great, and you know what you're doing … I know, but, as my grandfather used to say, "just keep living, then you'll find out". And we all soon find out, don't we? We find out that our intentions aren't always pure, our patience needs work, our perspective needs some alterations and our grace needs greater capacity. Admitting such things is scary to do, but therein lies the strength of honesty and the opportunity to cultivate a good marriage.

It was in my second year of marriage when I began to have some honest conversations with myself. Through a series of circumstances, I had to face the difficult truth that I suffered from severe selfishness and that it needed to be addressed. It prevented me, on several levels, from having consistent grace for Jarrett and his needs. Extra time was about me, extra money was about me, schedules, plans, arguments … it was all about me and though I felt sincere about growing and building a good home and connecting with Jarrett on deeper levels, I must admit that the underlying reasons were for my personal benefit. I knew that loving involved doing good for another person, but God's love and His conviction began to show me that loving well means doing good with my husband, rather than for him. This was my first personal challenge in marriage. It was uncomfortable and difficult, but it paved the way for honesty and maturity and a greater disposition to love well.

The Bible tells us that those who get married will face trials in their lives (1 Corinthians 7:28). Yes, even good marriage will have problems – some that occur from outside circumstances and some that occur from within. But, in your trials, you can still have a strong, loving and prosperous marriage, just as you would on the days you enjoy hot sex and white sandy beaches. A good marriage is about living well and loving well and this must be done together, not as thoughtful favors, but as a unified life. Challenges will come, but truthfulness in conjunction with those conflicts create incredible growth that your marriage will benefit from.

Marriage is a precious gift from the Lord's heart, and He doesn't give us His heart in pieces. His gifts are eternal and true and good and given with your heart in mind and I firmly and strongly believe that your husband was given to you and you were given to him because God loves you both unconditionally and desires to use your marriage to confirm this truth to each other and to the whole world. This is the mission of marriage: to love one another as Christ has loved us and to reflect His truth in our daily living. Thisrequires honest moments where we choose to face personal imperfections while leaning on the redemptive love of Jesus, which will build our capacity to extend grace to our husbands while growing in grace with our Lord. It's all a process towards producing unconditional intimacy, trust, oneness and fidelity and it demands more than any human being possesses on their own. It requires the love of God, which is always constant and perfect and true.

In marriage, we know there are many lessons, lots of messes, confessions and personal transformations that we must endure as we seek The Lord and become changed by Him in pursuit of commissioning a beautiful life of love. It's a process in our lives and it's also a process in our marriages. A good marriage can only be built on the truth, not in denial or pretension. It's in the growing and becoming seasons where transformation takes place to propel our marriages and mature our love beyond self-centered ambitions and momentary feelings. Admitting that we need to grow more and become more is vulnerable and scary, but this, my friend, is true strength and when we allow our walls of self-preservation to come crumbling down, we enable our hearts the oxygen it needs to beat and breathe. The exposed cracks of our humanity will then allow us to peer into the hearts of our husbands and permit them to gaze into ours, as well. The challenge is in the choosing to do so. Building better love is all about our choices for truth, not our circumstances we may be tempted to hide. It's not easy all the time but living transparent lives with one another can reposition where we currently are and direct our marriages further into where we need them to be.

Reactions and Results

Loving well won't stop the messes. Misunderstandings, problems, apologies ... these are all part of life and of marriage. I should know, because I wear the crown of mess ups! Let me give you an example. A few nights ago, I was late with dinner and my daughters were going crazy! They had recently figured out how to unlock the back door and were running in and out of the house, running past me to open the refrigerator, tripping me up between the stove, the pantry and the kitchen sink. Our baby girl was grabbing at my pants and crying for me to pick her up, but I couldn't. I was deep in dirty dishes, trying to prepare a scrumptious dish for diner. Midway into my preparations, I realized the tomato I had in the fridge went bad. Actually, it stunk, and as I was on my way to toss it in the trash can, one of my daughters zoomed under my legs, causing me to drop the squishy fruit - splattering rotten tomato all on the floor. If you know me, you already know what I did ... I cried. I just cried! Compelled and concerned, my sweet girls instantly ran to hug me, grabbing me at the knee which caused me to lose my balance and fall over them. This was the scene that Jarrett walked in on: his daughters hanging onto their crying mother who was sitting in the middle of the floor, stained with tomato juice! Nice, right?

In that moment, all I wanted was for him to scoop me up in his arms, away from the girls and the tomato and dinner and just give me one of his wonderful "Jarrett kisses". That's all I wanted. But it's not what I got. Instead, I got a laugh. He chuckled at the sight and it crushed me. It crushed me that he didn't react or respond the way I needed him to, and it hurt me that he couldn't sense how overwhelmed I felt and that I needed an immediate embrace. It crushed me that, after years of marriage, he could still be so unaware of how sensitive I am and, as a result, was unable to respond in the way that I desired him to.

"What happened here?", He asked me, smirking.

"Nothing", I said.

"What's wrong?", He asked, as I jolted upstairs.

Completely immature, I know, but my feelings got the better of me … again! Laid out across our bed, I felt all the emotions rush through my heart and my mind, and I realized that I had a choice. Seven years ago, I would have let my feelings lead me into whirlwinds of frustration, which would have resulted in my demanding that he be more sensitive and that laughing was rude and unappreciated. This would have resulted in him trying to defend himself and that would have resulted in me feeling that his defense was proof that he wasn't considering my feelings: the precise environment for an unnecessary argument and further hurtful feelings.

Playing that in my mind, I decided that I didn't want to go there this time. I decided that I didn't want to breed an argument. Instead, I would wait. I would use the few seconds of quiet time to whisper a heartfelt prayer to the Lord and tell Him all about it. I told Jesus that I was trying to make a pleasant dinner for my family and that it all went to hell in a hand basket and that Jarrett's reaction burned me deeper than the chicken that was probably scorching at this very moment. I told the Lord that I wished my husband had have run to my rescue, sensing my deepest need to have been reassured, affirmed and embraced. And then, I asked the Lord to please keep my heart from being angry so that I could love my husband in spite of my feelings. I asked Jesus to please protect my heart from offense so that our evening wouldn't be ruined by any internal negativity or unresolved perspectives on either of our accounts.

You see, that wasn't the first time my husband smirked at me. It tends to be his way of releasing his uncomfortable or shocked feelings. Some people's first reactions are to frown, or to cry or to show signs of agitation. Jarrett's first reactions usually involve laughing. He laughs when the girls fall and bump their heads. He laughed when I hit the neighbor's mailbox with the car. He snickered when his mom fell and had to get a boot put on her leg. I'm not sure why, but that's just his way. I hate it. It's one of those things that truly annoys me and, unfortunately, I am guilty of accusing him of not caring, even though I know he does. It's just not how I would respond to distress, and therefore, I wish he wouldn't respond in ways that I don't like. But I am learning that grace, like offense, is a choice and the results of my reactions can be harnessed by simply choosing to respond graciously instead of grueling him for reacting differently than I would.

Conflicts are commonly among us, but they don't have to control us. I knew I could focus on what I didn't like and punish him for it, or I could consider his heart – that he loves me – and I could choose to give him grace and give my hurt feelings to the Lord. So that's what I did and no sooner had I prayed that, I heard big feet walking up the steps and then I felt a huge warm body lay over me in a total and complete embrace.

"I'm sorry I laughed and hurt your feelings. I cleaned up the girls. Dinner smells great. "

And just like that, I received the embrace my heart was longing for as well as help, affirmation and a compliment! I didn't have to point any fingers or tell him about himself. I didn't have to lash out or over dramatize the situation. He gave freely from his heart, because he loves me deeply. Your husband loves you deeply, too.

I want to challenge you to consider your husband's heart and contemplate your choices when it comes to your reactions. Are you giving him the opportunity to show you that he loves you deeply? Are you giving him grace and space to approach you and to make things right with you? You have the authority over your reactions to build better love by doing the loving thing. Sometimes, this means being silent in our waiting (Proverbs 15:1), to ponder or to pray. It's always far better to listen with love than to burst out in irritation, offense or blame. This will never draw you closer together – with your husband or with anyone else, for that matter. It might feel strong in the moment, but it won't result in better love. The Bible tells us that those who use grace are wise, but anyone who lashes out in rage is stupid (Proverbs 14:29). Harsh words, I know, but a tempter renders harsh results because it produces separation. Hindered hearts have no harmony. We have to choose carefully how we respond and react, because the results will take its toll on your evening, on your week and evenly possibly your lives.

Rituals to Make (And Keep)

Building better love in our marriages can be simple to accomplish. Your love can be forever blessed with lessons to learn and treasures to keep! But this looks different for everyone. Some marriages enjoy regular get-a-ways in far off sunny places. Some marriages include the rapidity of working out together in order to serve as each other's motivation and support. Other marriages include eating meals together every day in order to share time and space and the joy of good food. Whatever your interests may be, I think it goes a long way to create and include consistent rituals and habits to share with one another in order to build better love.

What are some things that you and your husband do, every day, together without fail? If you take the time to consider, you may recognize patterns that are unique to your relationship. Maybe it occurred by happenstance, maybe my intentions, but developing positive and loving rituals within your marriage can certainly aid in building better love between the two of you because it contributes to your oneness and identity as a couple and as lovers.

According to Dr. Ryan and Selena Frederick, authors of *Fierce Marriage*, small moments of regular connection, like spending time or using physical touch and eye contact, can go a long way in creating and sustaining a healthy bond. "Rituals will help you connect and increase the security and safety of (your marriage). They are ways of saying "you matter to me" and "we matter to each other."[2] Of all the amazing rituals that you could (and should) be creating, an amazing one that I'd like to suggest is the incorporation of greeting and parting rituals. Basically, this is how you say, "hello" and "goodbye". Besides just being cordial, this can radically increase some lovely passion that each of you can look forward to throughout your day!

In the morning, it's so easy to get swept up with your day before it even begins. We are all guilty of scrolling through our feed before our feet hit the floor sometimes. Maybe you have linked your emails to your phone and start your morning right off the bat checking your calendars or notes. These aren't bad things, but they could steal precious moments to jumpstart your passion with one another! I'd like to suggest that you don't forsake your "Honeymoon Mornings". That's what Jarrett calls them! It's when you take the first few moments of your morning, as you both are waking up, to share a pillow and a smile and just breathe each other in! It's that place between asleep and awake where tiny flirts can flame some sensual responses and intimate moods. Weather this leads to something more is up to the two of you, but it definitely helps kickstart a great day!

When it comes to parting for the day and going your separate ways, creating a farewell that is intentional can do so much good for you both. I know for us, a quick kiss just won't do.

---

[2] Frederick, R., & Frederick, S. *Fierce marriage: Radically Pursuing Each Other in Light of Christ's Relentless Love.* Baker Publishing Group, 2018.

We make it a point to embrace and pray before either of us leave the house for the day. This has been such a regular practice between us that our youngest daughter has made it her personal agenda to see to it that we don't miss a day of this. On days when either Jarrett or I feel rushed, Jaelle will stop us right there in our tracks! She knows our ritual and notices if we miss step. Both of our girls have no problem holding us accountable because they've observed how important and consistent it has been in our home.

Greeting and leaving each other for the day or for extended periods of time can set the stage for the entire time spent apart as well as for the return. I'd like to encourage you to carve out intentional moments to embrace each other and wish each other a beautiful day, because every day is a gift and a blessing

(Psalms 118:24). These are simple measures everyone can take to intentionally show love and produce results that can add to your passion and your intimate exchanges with one another. It says a lot more than rushing past each other in efforts to do things that are not as valuable. There is no other time spent that is more important than the time that you spend together. This is how love (and babies) are made! As you examine some of your current habits and rituals, take a closer look at any area that may not be beneficial to your desire to love well. Life is short and time is few. Build better love needs to be encouraged and nurtured and fanned into flame. It only takes a little intentionality to build better love. The rituals you set with each other can do more for you throughout your day and your night!

True Strength Gives Grace

I know our culture tells us that women run the world and that we must exercise our voice and our feelings, no matter what. But if we are not careful, we can easily mistake an outburst for strength or our right to be heard as a precedence over our God-given gift to be loving. Never forget that you are in control of your reaction and you alone are responsible for your responses. It's a lack of patience and self-control that produces negative outbursts or undermining statements (Proverbs 14:29). Your response is always your choice. A woman who desires to love well knows that loving well requires choosing well. Reactions are a choice, so choose who is in control: you or your feelings?

Patience is beautiful and grace is strength. As we become more intentional about building better love, we find that grace is not just an option, it's a treasure. My marriage is teaching me so much about grace giving. I've failed tremendously at being gracious over the course of seven years, but the tomato situation is just one of many little moments that have taught me what true strength is all about. It's not about forcing the other person to agree with us or manipulating a conversation so that we receive apologies. It's about extending love to strengthen our marriages and produce restorative outcomes. Grace is powerful! Grace is loving! We hear this word so often within the Christian community that it has become common verbiage that's not always applied. It gets inserted into sermons, songs and books ... even this book, but I want to be sure that we all truly understand what the word means – not just it's definition, but also its implication, because, when applied, grace changes everything.

According to the Baker's Evangelical Dictionary of Biblical Theology, grace is producing goodness to someone who deserves punishment[3]. It's a withholding of revenge and a pouring out of blessings, instead of penalties. Think about that for a moment. Based on this description, grace is even greater than forgiveness. To forgive means to no longer hold a personal grudge, while still administering reprimands to the guilty. Grace is extremely different because it not only forgives the offense; it releases the person from the obligation of paying for that offense. This is the power of the Gospel and the Love of Christ, but it's also the missing element in so many marriages; maybe even yours.

Grace is a necessity to harmony. It's a cure for resentment and an invitation to restoration. We are all guilty in some form or fashion. Maybe you are guilty of being a mean person. Maybe you are guilty of putting harmful things into your body. Maybe you have lied or live in selfishness or use profanity in your conversations. Maybe you've been an unloving wife or even an unloving person. You're not alone. Those who are guilty, say, "I"! That means all of us, because all of us are sinners (Romans 3:23). Sin isn't just bad things done or said, it's whatever is outside of God's love. This includes thoughts not acted upon, lifestyles that we excuse for our

---

[3] Elwell, Walter A. *Evangelical Dictionary of Biblical Theology*. Baker Books, 2001.

own pleasures, feelings that inflame us and daydreams that overtake us. Anything we experience that does not reflect the holiness of God is sin and we are all guilty of this. But there is hope! It's not in a vacation, in more sex (or less sex), it's not in raises or paid bills or new furniture or more children. Grace is found in only one source. His name is Jesus!

Truth be told, marriage certainly has a way of placing us in situations where our shortcomings become magnified. The daily opportunity to extend grace never gets easier as we continue to live together with our imperfect husbands and families. We see our man's struggles, shortcomings and flaws and they see ours. There is no space for hiding; not really. We are totally exposed and effected by the humanity we carry and therefore have some decisions to make. Do we punish our husbands for hurting our feelings or do we give grace? Do we blame and point fingers for bad choices or inconsiderate behavior, or do we give grace? In a nutshell, do we choose our self-centered rights or do we choose the grace of Jesus? Do we choose the better thing? The stronger thing?

It's easy to hold someone accountable and responsible for their wrongdoing because we are people of pride and of principle. We want to be treated the way we like being treated and we don't want to give off a sense that we are weak. This might feel strong — like we aren't allowing someone to get over on us or take advantage of us, but this isn't strength at all. It's hypocrisy, because we are always just as guilty as everyone else. Grace is greater! It's what separates a flourishing marriage from the basic ones and it's what will transform tension into testimonies!

Listen, it's easy to let someone have it. It's easy to hold someone responsible for their mistakes and unfavorable behaviors. You have the right to do this and still be forgiving, but that will not build better love; it will hinder it. The Bible tells us that a foolish person expresses their anger in full measure (Proverbs 29:11), but love covers a multitude of sins (1 Peter 4:8). Grace is loving. Grace is not excusing the problem, rather it is extending the opportunity to begin again without the burden of demanding that someone has to prove or earn their chance to start over. Demanding explanations and apologies or worse, rejecting explanations or refusing to accept apologies is not the love of Christ. It isn't strength and it will foolishly sabotage a life of harmony, unity and relationship. Such things are hindrances to loving well and the result is strain and stress and separation, which all produce negative ramifications, not always immediately, but most assuredly in the future.

Everything I'm sharing is coming from personal experience. I'm not talking over you or pointing my finger at you. I'm sitting beside you, with intense eyes and a heart full of hope for you because I'm also learning that grace is a powerful foundation. When I think about the tomato situation, I realize it could have become a very negative story if grace hadn't been administered. But grace changes the story every time. When we pair that with patience, we can see God's hand working out miracles, both big and small. It's a choice and I want you to start choosing grace. I want you to stop reading books that don't point you to grace. I want you to stop singing songs that tell you strength lies in rejection or vengeance, power or control. These are lies and all lies come from hell. Rejection tears down and vengeance destroys second chances. Exerting our power makes others feel small. This is not God's love; therefore, it is not God's best over you or for your marriage.

On the contrary, grace creates fertile love and it blooms strength within our marriages, our relationships with others and even the relationship with ourselves. It's the grace of God that made relationship with Jesus possible (Ephesians 2: 8-9)! Since grace is so life changing for our souls, think about what it can do for our marriages! There is always enough grace to go around, minute to minute, and what God gives to us, we should give to others rather than withholding it simply because things done or said didn't cater to our preferences. Instead, giving grace looks like having vulnerable and honest conversations so that you can understand the intentions of the other person and maturely express your perspective and your feelings. Grace looks like reaching out, intentionally, rather than rejecting out of fear or immaturity. Grace looks like admitting you were wrong, on the spot, rather than choosing your pride by avoiding or excusing your responsibilities in a matter. Show me an ungracious person, and I will show you someone who is afraid, insecure and weak. Show me a quick-tempered person and I will show you a person who is fearful, intimidated and cowardly.

The greatest example of a lack of grace is found in a story Jesus told, about a man who was pardoned a great debt that he could not repay. He was wrong and irresponsible and therefore was at the mercy of the king. His fate was prison, but the king, out of his strength, gave the man grace and freedom by erasing his debt. Leaving such a heavy load behind him and reentering the world as a free man, he came across a neighbor who owed him a few dollars. Enraged, the man instantly forgot about his own forgiven debt and seized his neighbor, demanding that he repay him all that he owed. Out of his weakness, the man demanded payment, though he himself had just received a pardon. When the king heard about this situation, he was greatly offended by the man's lack of grace towards his neighbor. The man was arrested immediately; never to enjoy freedom again.

This story can be found in Matthew 8: 21-35. It's such an incredible depiction of our eternal situation. Yes, we can demand our payment, our apology and our right to be upset, but the loving thing is to give grace. Outbursts and rejection are the response of the insecure and of the emotionally weak. Mean words, the silent treatment, cruel behaviors and payback is a lack of grace and therefore, a lack of love. As women who desire to love well, these things have no place in our lives, let alone our marriages. I get how frustrating it can be to feel misunderstood or unconsidered. I know that disappointments take their toll on all of us in different ways. This can produce insecurities within us, which can cause us to hide behind the false image of strength. Many of us are afraid of being perceived as weak, but the power of this world is not a reflection of the graciousness and gentle spirit that we should be carrying (James 1:20; 1 Peter 3:4).

Had I demanded that apology from Jarrett instead of giving my feelings to Jesus, the tomato wouldn't have been the only thing smashed that night. Sadly, I can recount many stories in my marriage where grace wasn't given in fear that it would make me look weak. But what I'm realizing is that when our messages get lost in translation or if our husbands don't respond in ways that we wish they naturally would, it's more productive to pray about it. On the spot. In our hearts. Before we respond. This way, we are trusting our Heavenly Father to make all things right so that nothing interrupts our ability to give or receive gracious love.

Listen, no man wants a confrontational wife. No man wants a wife who's constantly going to war with him. He will either engage in defense or shut down in defeat. But you already know this, don't you? You've already seen him walk out of the room or roll over in bed. That's not what either of you want. You have a lot of influence to change the situation. You have a lot of sway to prevent hostility. It's all in how you choose to handle it. It has nothing to do with the condition of your marriage because your marriage is above your circumstances. Even in the arguments, conflicts and misunderstand-- ings, you can deal in loving and gracious ways. You can choose to use grace in the midst of hurt feelings and disagreements. The Bible calls this having a quiet and gentle spirit (Colossians 3:12) and it shows great beauty as well as self-control and strength.

Scripture isn't demanding that we shut up and do as we're told. On the contrary! We are better apt to make wise decisions and suggestions when we are quiet, calm and gentle. A gracious attitude is more attractive than a hostile one or an intolerant one. True strength gives grace (Matthew 26:63). It reaches out and offers opportunity to resolve and restore. It's a reflection of the Gospel, which is the heart of God and it is a powerful, life changing and mission driven virtue. It allows us to ponder and think and pray and wait and it's always in the waiting where the answers are revealed. It takes patience to listen and grace to learn. I'm not always successful in remembering this in the moment, but when I do, it makes for much better love! That's all I want for my marriage – better love, fuller love, a love that's not constantly interrupted by frustrations, or tension. I truly want to love in ways that represent the love of Christ, don't you?

<u>Truth and Tributes</u>

Let's be honest, we all have come short of loving well in some Form or fashion, but this doesn't define our value or the cherished love God desires for our marriages. Building better love requires God's love and His truth, rather than our striving. Outside of Him, we're left with our inconsistent efforts which are incapable of maintaining unconditional love. Marriage was meant for more than this. Your marriage was meant for more than make up sex or cordial toleration. Its essence was meant to remind you of the Gospel and to mirror the power of God's unconditional love for us all, through Christ (John 3:16). Without knowing His love, there is no way you will be able to extend it in your marriage. A relationship with Jesus changes us and changed people produce changed outcomes. Trust the Lord and let go of power; give grace and let Christ help you build better love. I desire this so much for myself, as well as for you. My prayer for all of us is to awaken to the truth that demands us to dig deeper and develop further into the women God has called us to be through the power and promise of Christ's Salvation and His unfailing love. His truth always calls for us to examine our hearts, confess our errors, extend grace and align our lives with His Word. Building better love cannot take place outside of truth and it won't last long based on feelings and emotions. We need the Lord and we need His truth to produce in our marriages what feelings simply cannot.

Becoming truth tellers and truth seekers is vital for the sake of our marriages and for the benefit of becoming women who love well. Yes, there are disappointments and things we've experienced that we didn't sign up for. Yes, you both have made mistakes and will continue to do so. But that does not define or determine whether or not you're in a good marriage. You determine whether or not you're in a good marriage and the course you set must be guided by God, not your feelings. Your marriage is not your sole responsibility, so tribute your husband in his efforts to love you well and resolve to grow together! Always remember that your marriage was made possible because of the man that you married. You wouldn't be married without him, so give him tribute as you both seek the Lord in navigate what loving well is all about.

Through the course of these pages, I want to give tribute to my husband and to his love and role in our marriage; not because we are the perfect couple, but because we choose to love each other through the perfect love of Jesus, and we choose to be honest with ourselves on how we are loving one another. Quite often, we have intentional moments when we ask each other how we are doing in loving one another. Jarrett will ask me, "how happy are you with how I've been loving you? Is there something I'm missing?". In turn, I will answer honestly and then ask him the same questions and we will then celebrate and give tribute to one another for the ways in which we have been loving and supporting and helping each other. It's an intense conversation, because it requires honesty and vulnerability, but truth isn't something we should ever be afraid of. It lights our path and guides us in the way that we need to go. Avoiding the truth is avoiding growth and a marriage that is not growing is a marriage that is not thriving. The truth can be scary to say and to receive, but it's is vital for building better love. I want to build with Jarrett and his commitment to build with me is something that I honor and I esteem greatly! I so desire to keep this at the center of who we are as a couple and who I am as a woman. Jesus tells us that He is the way, the truth and the life (John 14:6). All truth points us to Jesus and I desire all that the presence of the Lord brings because it has made all the difference for us.

Scripture tells us that God is love and that loving others, purely, cannot take place without a relationship with Him (1 John 4:16). This is the truth, and this is the Gospel, so we must give God tribute to His love over us and attribute our love for one another to the fact that God loved us first (1 John 4:19). It's His love that builds better love in our lives. This doesn't mean that the presence of God removes difficulties or disappointments from our marriages, but it does mean that the peace and perfection of His presence will empower and equip us to love in inconceivable ways, in spite of disappointments or unpredictable outcomes.

I believe without a doubt that you have chosen this book because you do desire to be a woman who loves well. You want your marriage to thrive and flourish, in and out of season. You desire to cultivate a love that lasts beyond the butterflies and beyond the temporary comforts of our society. This is how I desire to love my husband, as well. I want to love him even when I'm pissed at him. I want to take good care of his heart, even when I don't agree with him. I want to forgive all his flaws, any of his insensitivities, every misunderstanding, every let down … all of it. I want to also celebrate all of his accomplishments, all of his growth, every opportunity that comes into his life, raise his babies, be his "good thing"
(Proverbs 18:22) and support his vision with earnest prayer and godly wisdom. I know this is what you want, too. In order for this to happen, we must resolve in our hearts to entrust our love to the Lord because a thriving and flourishing marriage is a tribute to God. It takes the presence of the Lord to be forgiving, to be gracious and to be unconditional in our loving. As wives, we need to be able to love our men in this way because we've already established that they are not perfect. Imperfect people do imperfect things. That's life and

that's marriage, but our hope rises above our imperfections because they do not define us.

I'm giving us all permission to stop expecting perfection in our marriages, in our husbands and even in ourselves. A problem-free marriage is impossible. What is possible, however, is to daily practice the perfect love of Christ by welcoming the presence of the Lord into our marriages and attributing His faithfulness into our love. This is done by inviting the Lord into your life and including Him into the development and circumstances of your marriage. No one can ever know the fullness of what's in your heart, but the Lord does. No other person can perceive the essence of your greatest needs except God. Just give your marriage and yourself to Him and watch Him work in both of you and see His plans for your marriage unfold in the daily living and loving between you and your husband. This is how we build better love with our husbands: we choose to give grace rather than prove a point. We are honest and gracious by trusting them to be the men we married, we position ourselves to receive their efforts to love us, and we invite the Lord into all the moments in between. We give tribute to their love because they are our gifts and we give tribute to the Lord for giving us the treasure of marriage. The sooner we divorce this notion that our marriages shouldn't be difficult or that disappointment in marriage is unforgiveable, the sooner we can move into truly cultivating love that goes deeper than rudimentary romance and last longer than petty little complements.

This is How We Build

Several kisses, and reassurances later, I returned downstairs to see that the tomato was cleaned up and there was a bag of Lindt Caramels on the table that Jarrett had brought home for me. My absolute favorites! In my distress, I hadn't even noticed the bag in his hand when he came home. Impatience costs us blessings. There is no way to see what God is offering us when we are too quick to respond to how we feel instead of pressing into what His Spirit desires to reveal. I'm very thankful for that experience because it taught me not only the power of grace giving, but how patience allows us to see more clearly when we pray and seek the Lord, rather than seeking opportunities to defend ourselves or speak our mind. Marriage is about love given and love received. So, this is how we build: by patiently choosing the opportunity to be loving and to give grace. We can grow deeper with one another and with the Lord in this way.

It's an exchange of our lives, our hearts and our souls. Anything that would threaten the spiritual harmony and unity in our marriages just isn't worth it. This includes our emotions. I'm praying we begin to ask the Lord to make us women who are patient and kind with beautiful spirits and flowering grace. Personally, I want to be a wife who goes to the Lord instead of going for the verbal punch. A broken face isn't pretty, neither is a broken man. We have the privilege and responsibility to build our husbands up by simply allowing them opportunities to be loving towards us in their own way, rather than condescending them simply because they did not respond to our preference. Remember, they are learning, too, and they want to do a good job of loving you, just as you desire to love them! So, let's trust their hearts and give them the grace that we all need, daily. Let's build better love by actually being loving and watch our marriage flourish as a result! This will make us better wives, better women and better people, all in this one lesson! Building anything takes intentionality. When we find ourselves in conflicts where our emotions are raging war against our willingness to be loving, that is the perfect time to choose grace to build and allow the Lord to guide us so that our marriages are enhanced in spite of the disturbance; not hindered by it.

Reflection

Where are some areas in your life that you can implement more grace towards your husband in order to build better love?

<u>Scriptures for Your Soul</u>

"A soft answer turns away wrath, but a harsh word stirs up anger."
- Proverbs 15:1 (ESV)

"You then, be strengthened by the grace that is in Christ Jesus."
- 2 Timothy 2:1 (ESV)

CHAPTER 2

THE DESIGN FOR MARRIAGE

"In sickness and in health, 'til death should separate us."

I remember speaking those words, seven years ago. Jarrett looked so dapper in his suit and tie! He held my hand so tenderly as my Father presided over our ceremony. Family and friends surrounded us, and prayer covered us. I gave him my forever heart as we pledged covenant vows to each other. Oddly enough, in my white gown, hand made by my Mother, death was the furthest thing from my mind. So was sickness, poverty and any other troubling experience. I wasn't thinking about the bad times on my wedding day. I don't know many brides who do. Of course, I aspire to be a realist like most of us, and I know that the sun doesn't shine continuously. But on that first day of June and filled with elation, I had no consideration of the rain.

Swept away in the joy of my new matrimony, my heart was bursting with hope and expectation. There was no invitation or consideration for fear or doubt or worry. Everything was right that day and everyone was happy. But happiness and excitement are never constant in life, any more than summer days and sunny skies. It's not a constant in anyone's marriage, either. The rain will one day come, as sure as the sunshine. Troubling experiences will eventually visit us all, no matter how in love you are. But the more I am married, the more I realize that God's design for marriage was never meant for our continual happiness; it was meant to serve as a platform in which He can perform His holiness.

The reality is that it takes both rain and sunshine to grow gardens; you can't expect to have the joy of the harvest without the pain of the pruning. It's a sobering thought, I know, but it isn't real love if you're unwilling to go through problems together. It's all part of God's design for love that is true, not just good. Nobody wants that, though. Nobody wants to suffer or be inconvenienced or be corrected or deal with problems or challenges of any kind. Sad to say, our culture doesn't prepare us to handle the trials of life in our marriages. Culture tells us exactly the opposite of what scripture instructs when it comes to true love.

"Love bears all things, believes all things, hopes all things, endures all things."
-1 Corinthians 13:7 (ESV)

True love endures all things. All things. It's not a

commonly practiced virtue in our society, but when placed in God's hands, it's absolutely possible! Whether you are happily married in this moment or going through some growing pains and challenges, I'm here to encourage you that this does not inhibit God's design for marriage in your life; it's a part of that design. Successful marriages, where love is strong and true, aren't built on the swaying emotions of happiness or the glutton of personal satisfaction. There is so much more involved in the process of cultivating lasting and enduring love. Commitments are for calendars, but covenants take a marriage higher and deeper and richer in God's design. A woman who desires to love well is ready to love, fully, no matter what the seasons of life may choose to impose upon her because she understands that covenant in her marriage is sacred to God.

Covenants and Contracts

I've heard the argument that people don't need a piece of paper to show they love someone. It's a good argument, in my opinion, when you're talking about the act of generally loving others. I don't need a piece of paper to prove to my mother that I love her. I don't need a signed document to prove that I love my children or my brother or my best friends. But those relationships aren't spiritual, and neither are they sexual. Marriage is unique from any other relationship because it invokes covenant which requires the exchanging of vows and oaths to God, first and foremost, and then to one another.

Promises today are nothing like the sacred practice of covenants exchanged in the era of the Old Testament. According to Strong's Concordance, a covenant involved a life or death agreement sealed by blood [4]. Those walking into the covenant were fully aware that it's weight would endure their whole lives long, but, if broken, it would be penalized by death. That's deeper than our modern day promises which often have escape clauses attached! Nowadays, people use their words to enter into a clausal contract, rather than extending their hearts into a covenant vow. We speak words with our fingers crossed behind our backs and write statements with loopholes in them. Words don't hold true weight anymore; they are no longer our bond. It's so common for people to make conditional promises, even in marriage; but in the days of Abraham, that would have been inadmissible because God was in the covenant. He still is!

In Genesis chapter 15, we see one of the first covenants exchanged between God and Abraham, sealing God to the people of Israel through an animal sacrifice. In the Gospels (Matthew, Mark, Luke and John) we see Jesus making a covenant to His people on the cross, through the shedding of His blood for all sins. Life and death are in a covenant. If we mark our births on paper and we mark our deaths on paper to prove it's officiality, it's quite reasonable

---

[4] Strong, J. *Strong's Exhaustive Concordance*. Peabody, MA: Hendrickson, 2007.

to mark our marriages on paper, for the same reasons. A covenant is life or death. Is your marriage life or death for you? Are you loving at all costs?

Other arguments oppose the tradition of marriage, as if tradition is proof that marriage is no longer necessary or relevant. But my argument lies in the belief that what has been passed down throughout the centuries very well proves its validity and value. History proves that marriages is an occurrence amidst every culture, worldwide, reaching back to eras past. This is something to take note of. Marriage should be held in honor by all (Hebrews 13:4). Even though the wedding ceremony and the exchanging of vows can be a traditional affair, God's design for marriage is deeper than mere tradition. Not everyone has an elaborate wedding day. Some people don't even have a formal ceremony and that's fine. That's not what marriage is about. Marriage is about covenant between one man and one woman. It's life changing and was meant to be life lasting.

"Therefore, a man shall leave his father and mother and hold fast to his wife, and the two shall become one flesh." This mystery is profound,

and I am saying that it refers to Christ and the church."

-Ephesians 5: 31-32 (ESV)

According to the Baker's Evangelical Dictionary of Biblical

Theology, the word "mystery" often refers to what was once unknown or unclear in the past but is now revealed to us through the Spirit.[5] All scripture is God-breathed (2 Timothy 3:16). This means that whatever is recoded in scripture is actually a revelation to us in areas we once were unaware of. This doesn't mean that we will understand everything in scripture, but it does mean that the Spirit of God has revealed Himself to us through the scriptures (2 Corinthians 2:10). "Mystery", therefore, is not a secret that is kept from us, but rather a truth that is reveled to us. So, the great mystery of marriage is that our union has been given to us as a gift in which we can portray to the world the unconditional and covenant love between Christ and the church –a love that we will spend our entire existence learning to understand. What a calling! It's definitely deeper than the swooning picture of "true love" the media tries to paint for us.

God's design for our marriages is a covenant, not a contractual agreement passed down through tradition. It's a spiritual gift made relevant in the natural occurrences of our lives. It's design was meant for a lifelong oath in which the Lord can use to teach us about His unconditional love for us and His grace over us (Ephesians 5:31-32). A woman who desires to love well understands that her marriage is a ministry and is commissioned for more than just emotional security or a comfortable partnership. Such frivolities are conveniences that

---

[5] Elwell, Walter A. *Evangelical Dictionary of Biblical Theology*. Baker Books, 2001.

fall underneath the criteria of contractual feelings, not covenant love. Instead, as wives whose hearts desire the Lord's favor, we have been called to greater. We have been entrusted to submit our love underneath the eternal love of Jesus which will direct our marriage deeper than a contract ever could.

The world waters this sacred design down to a false belief that marriage is simply an agreement between two consenting people and that, if for any reason either party sees fit, the contract can be terminated, and each can go their own way, unbound by the previous promises they made. But this is a cheap version of what God had in mind when He instituted marriage. Marriage is a physical illustration of a spiritual covenant made available through Salvation. God's plan for His relationship with us is to be binding, lifelong and eternally secure. It's not passive or momentary. It was designed to last forever, not because of feelings, but because of covenant.

Friends, marriage is missional and it's a calling. The true purpose positioned between the promises of our vows is covenant. If marriage is only based on a momentary agreement to an imperfect person, then the limitations of our own imperfections will eventually overtake any good intentions for the future. Since marriage is spiritual, we must align our hearts spiritually by understanding that our promises and vows were made to God, not just to another person. His design for marriage is in covenant — an eternal promise of unconditional love, which His Spirit produces and continuously rebirths within a Christ centered marriage.

I know that some of you may have experienced the sting of divorce in your life. Maybe personally or maybe through your parents or others in your intimate circle. The brokenness of divorce brings about devastating anguish. That's why God declares that He hates divorce (Malachi 2:16). He doesn't hate the people; he hates the decision. But even still, His love never fails (Psalm 136: 1-2). I may not understand the pain of such an experience, but I do know that restoration is God's design, too. He desires to restore every broken, grieving or angry heart. His love can restore marriages that are willing to be re-birthed. He can restore wounds from broken vows and prepare hearts for future ones. If divorce is a part of your story, take comfort and encouragement in knowing that in no way does this jeopardize God's covenant with you. His promises are never broken, and His presence is always with us.

Choosing First and Forever

We know God's design for marriage is not in the feelings, but good feelings are a part of a good life! It's a thrill to be loved and to return that love back, but realize that love is an action, not a sensation. Think back to your first kiss together – tingly and exciting and wonderful! No matter when you shared that first kiss with your husband, I know the thought of it puts a smile on your face! I remember our first kiss! Jarrett had taken me home from church. We were 23 years old without any concerns for the future. College life was behind us, but we hadn't truly become grownups yet. It was a sweet time for me, full of aspirations and questions and hopes for the future. Walking me to my apartment, the conversation began to trail off as we just stood there in the doorway. Jarrett leaned in for a hug and then went for it, as if he had been planning that kiss all day! It took me by such surprise! It was all I could think about for days and we made it a point to keep practicing!

Fast forward these many years later, I realize that it's important to remember moments like that - moments where the two of you share memories that only the two of you made. This puts intentionality at the forefront. Love isn't something we fall into, it's something that we cultivate and grow; it's an action and it's a choice. See, there is no other person on this earth that has permission to kiss me, to swoon me or to intimately embrace me, except Jarrett, because I chose for him to be. Every decision which lead up to our marriage was a choice. How sad when love becomes routine after the marriage has taken place. How even more sad when it becomes an irritation.

Too many times, we are guilty of forgetting the intentionality required for loving one another. It goes beyond the day in and day out of predictable patterns and monotonous moments. The choice of loving well, by implementing the unconditional love of God, should produce more than casual passion. Instead, our intentionality can ignite flames of purpose, vision and mission beyond basic sensuality.

Anything designed was done so with a purpose. The love between you and your husband has a purpose in God's design for your lives. Accepting that purpose and intentionally living out that purpose are two different decisions. We can accept that something is true without actually applying that truth. So, I ask you, are you being intentional in the way you are choosing to love? Is it a true depiction of God's design for marriage? There are too many of us who don't know what marriage is really about. We think it's about the anticipations associated with our first kiss. But I'm here to share with you that marriage is about the choice of our first kiss. It's about the choice to not only make love, but to be love because God is love (1 John 4:8). It's the choice to try, the choice to be open to one another and the choice to build each other up. It is a sacred calling to love without limits and to cherish one another as we should cherish our Creator, who designed marriage to be a reflection of His love for us.

The Proof

Feelings are real and valid and wonderful and there's no wrong in that, but these feelings aren't proof of love. The proof of love is the decision for loving and the intentional living. Our motives fuel the intentionality behind our choices. Marriage is a mutually satisfying existence, but if the motivation for our love is for ourselves, we've lost sight of the Gospel and we've lost sight of loving well. Self is a gluten. It doesn't see anything but its own pleasure; it doesn't consider anyone but itself. It has no vision for the future, only demands for the now. It's greedy, discontented, unreliable and hypocritical. Self only wants immediate gratification, comfort and pleasure. The problem with this is that no person on this earth can keep you happy all the time. If your love is only based on your personal contentment and emotional comforts, what happens when life challenges your comfort? If you married because he made you feel good, what happens when he does something that makes you feel bad? Notice, I'm using the word "when" not "if", because, in due time, we will all eventually become a challenge to one another; it's the unavoidable reality of imperfect people living in a fallen world. No one can keep anyone contented all the time. No one can fulfill the deepest longings of our hearts or meet the depths of our souls on a yearly, weekly or daily basis. The only hope for that is in the Gospel and the only way to apply the Gospel is through Jesus. He is the only One who has ever proved true love and His love is the only that can provide true love in your life and in your marriage.

Your spouse's ability to constantly recreate your first feelings of fresh romance is not their responsibility in cultivating or proving love in your life. That's a performance based perspective and performance is never unconditional. Performance places our relationships in obligation: unless you do this, I won't do this. If you do this, then I will do this. That type of arrangement is rooted in selfishness and does not depict the design of love and marriage that God desires to implement in your life. Ladies, ultimatums in exchange for love is not love. That isn't only selfish, it's immature, unspiritual and exhausting! No encore can last forever, no matter how many roses you throw on stage. No man can affirm your self-esteem, your securities or your feelings all the time. His ability (or inability) to keep you happy, sexy and slayed every day isn't proof of anything. That's not his responsibility to you and it's not your responsibility to him, either. More than anything, the proof of love is that you prioritize loving first, regardless of your feelings because God designed marriage to represent Himself.

Listen, your marriage to your husband is about him, not you. Your marriage to your man is about sharing and showing him the love of Christ in all your moments, motives and choices. We have to allow the Holy Spirit to shift our focus from our feelings to their needs. We must start exploring how can we serve them, instead of judging how they are serving us. We should be reflecting on ways we can love our husbands more, rather than how to get them to be more loving to us. It seems one sided, but if both spouses operate with this focus, no one is left wanting. This is God's design for marriage: to put the other's needs before our own in genuine and unconditional ways and to honor the Lord in our efforts and choices to love one another as He loves us. It starts with your daily choices and it's your choices that prove your love. The notion that marriage should be a continuous state of happily ever after just isn't realistic. It's immature and it's self-centered. Marriage isn't about you.

Marriage isn't about your personal happiness or your feelings; it's about God using the life of another person to draw you into deeper understanding of your need for His holiness in your life. He uses the hard things to show us our short comings and point us into the life changing truth of the Gospel and of Salvation.

Our capacity to love well falls completely dependent on knowing the love of Jesus Christ and this involves us understanding that we are continuously in need of the unconditional love of the Lord. We must possess His love if we are to live it out. That's the Gospel. It doesn't always feel good and it doesn't always give us tingling sensations or butterflies, but it will elevate the existence of your marriage into more purpose and meaning, beyond the emotions and above the feelings.

Sex and emotions and feelings and intimacy are all wonderful and vital and they have their place, but they do not prove love. Scripture makes it very clear that the love of God, which we should be experiencing in our marriages, is much more than emotional or physical feelings. Love is a commandment which we must obey, and Jesus said it's the greatest (1 Corinthians 13:13). Conflict doesn't exempt us. Rough seasons won't excuse us. Love is an action and it's also a choice.

"I give you a new commandment—to love one another. Just as I have loved you, you also are to love one another. Everyone will know by this that you are my disciples—if you have love for one another."
-John 13:34-35 (ESV)

The longer I am married the more I consider that God's truest intent and design for marriage is to produce greater godliness within us and point others to the Gospel. This Gospel is not about feeling good all the time or managing to maintain surfaced passion or romantic feelings; it's about showing and sharing the love of Jesus, which is a fire that will never burn out! Going about the world's way of loving will not solidify spiritual love in your life. At best, it's limitations counterfeit a perception of love, which will eventually run out –leading us longing and lonely in the end. But, by laying down our lives as Christ did, living our love with intentionality for one another and persisting to love beyond simply pursuing good feelings, our marriages will thrive and flourish both in the natural and in the spiritual. This is the Gospel, and this is what a God-centered marriage looks like. It's in our relationship with Jesus that we begin to see what loving well in our marriages truly looks like. This begins with an experience of His love, as shown to us through the Gospel. It can't be forced, manipulated, faked or duplicated. It's a choice we make by accepting the love of Christ and then allowing His love to flow within us, through us and into our marriages and out into the world.

Foundations and Vacations

In the same way that we chose to marry, we must also choose to love who we've married, according to God's design. In marriage, we have a truer opportunity to give selflessly, to forgive continuously, to seek wisdom and to daily lay down our lives for our families. No person can do that, unconditionally, without the hand of God. It just isn't possible, because we are flesh and flesh is never consistent. But, as we draw close to Jesus, His Holy Spirit renews and reshapes our hearts to then love like Him because His love isn't something we can duplicate. It's a gift God carefully and spiritually crafts and reveals to us alongside other beautiful mysteries He unveils to our hearts through His Word. It's only His love that ignites ours to maintain the promises of covenant and resist any emotions that would try to take us under and equip us to love for the long haul, come what may, in sickness and in health, for richer or poorer, 'til death should separate us. The choice to keep these promises are only possible through the love of our promise keeping God.

Scriptures make it clear that the design for marriage is God inspired and that is incredible to me. It's amazing that God's love for us is so vast that He put us together with our men, not just to make babies, but to bear His name and live as His ambassadors in a world that is dying to know what true love is. It's a huge honor and an overwhelming idea that our marriage is meant to exemplify the Gospel. A marriage that is truly rooted in Christ will display a vibrant representation of this divine design of pure love, mutual mission and spiritual oneness (1 Cor. 12:13). I believe this requires us to speak of marriage with transparency. We can't expect to point to the Gospel if we are pointing to ourselves. Showing off the good times while hiding the bad doesn't reveal redemption or the unconditional love of Christ in our lives. The world is looking for something real. They can go to Instagram for images about vacations. They want to come to you for insights on building godly foundations.

It's like the parable Jesus told in the book of Matthew, about the two men who built their houses. Let's elaborate a bit and give them names: Dave and Jim. Each man decided to build a home on the beach. Dave began to build his house right away. He evened out his portion of land and started laying down the floors of his future home. His wife laid out on the beach, enjoying the waves and sun while he hammered and sawed. They invested more into the image of their home than in the building of it. Jim's development took a little longer. He also evened out his portion of land, however, he dug a bit deeper and laid a concrete foundation before laying down his floors. He and his wife worked side by side, hammering, drilling, and growing quite tired, together. As they worked, they talked and laughed and shared their dreams of the future. Jim would ask his wife to take a break so that she could enjoy the beach, but she refused. Working alongside her husband was invaluable to her. She grew callouses on her hands; he was scorched by the sun, but neither minded the discomfort of building their forever together. In time, their home was complete.

In the months to come, the beautiful beach endured its many storms, but one storm did its worse damage to Dave's home. It knocked the entire estate over. The shallow foundation was no match for the burst of violent and unpredictable winds.

The house just couldn't stand amidst the turbulence. Jim and His wife welcomed the weather-beaten couple in for safety and offered their neighbors the full extent of a helping hand.

"It's fine", Dave replied, "It was just for vacation anyway."

Though this story is often taught to emphasis Salvation, I'm using it as an example for marriage. To be clear, in order to have a marriage designed God's way, we need a foundation in His Salvation. Without it, how can we expect to experience His unconditional love throughout the storms of life? Jesus taught us that the wise man built his house upon the rock and the foolish man built his house upon the sand (Matthew 7: 24-27). Each man's efforts rendered completely different results. It's something I often think about as I am raising my family and cultivating my marriage. Am I intentionally building a foundation or am I more concerned about the momentary ease of appearing to have one? Eventually, all improper foundations fail, so what we are building on is of great importance concerning the future outcomes of our marriages, our families, our faith and our lives. If God has good works to produce through us in Christ Jesus (Ephesians 2:10), then we need Christ Jesus in order to produce those good works in our lives, in our marriages and in our world. So, I'd like to ask you, how is the good work of your marital house being built? Is it implementing God's design to last or is it just a vacation home? Is Christ the foundation or just the mat at the entry way? Is God and His Gospel at the center of your marriage, or is it only a theme that you hang up and take down, seasonally or conveniently?

In a world that declares they are Christians, what makes your life any different? What sets a part your marriage from those who are blindly going through the motions of appearance and performance-based love? These are such pertinent questions we must ask ourselves in order to discover what is true and then petition the Lord to renew, establish and make all things new. His blessings require more than façades (2 Timothy 3:5). He's looking for hearts who desire His love and who are willing to allow the foundation of their marriages to be rooted in Him, as He designed it to be from the very beginning.

Loving well costs more than décor. It requires selfless intentionality and sometimes, even a degree of discomfort. I know we all want contentment and good feelings. We all want to sip drinks on the beach and enjoy the sun and the waves. We want life to be easy. But, in our story, I find great intrigue in the woman who chose to build and work hard alongside her man. She wasn't satisfied in being catered to. She wanted to ensure that things were strong and done right, so she traded her comfort for callouses and found joy in working alongside her husband to produce the results they desired, together. This is a beautiful picture because this is the call and cost of cultivating a strong foundation. Praying isn't always effortless. Forgiving isn't always easy. Sacrificing self, seeking peace, giving grace and apologizing aren't always lovely things to do. Marriage is work and sometimes, it's hard work. God's love is what we all need in our marriage if we desire to last past the feelings because when the rush of emotions wane and the problems of life begin to crash around us, we need a firm foundation to stand on. We need Salvation and the infilling of God's unconditional love through the power of the Holy Spirit as declared by the Gospel. Loving God's way is challenging, but these challenges mature us and develop us beyond what pictures can capture or what captions can brag about. To run on mission in light of God's eternal and unconditional love will make all the difference! It's this mission that will not only lead you into deeper love with your husband, but also into deeper love with your Heavenly Father. He has deeper things for your marriage, and He is calling you out: out of the crowd, out of the deception, out of the selfishness and out of surfaced living. He has purpose and mission, according to His divine design for you. It will require you to grow in ways you were unaware of and it will stretch you in areas you think you cannot handle, but it will strengthen every relationship around you, particularly with God and most definitely in your marriage.

Décor Is Not Enough

I know we like to dream of the grandeur of marriage where men are wining and dining their wives, bringing home big pay checks, elaborate jewelry and whisking her off to expensive vacations. We see the social media influencers kissing their husbands under the Eiffel Tower with big rocks on their hands and a professional photographer at their feet. We famous couples in million-dollar mansions and red soled shoes with men who offer them credit cards and private planes. We see musicians and entertainers showing the public glimpses of what they do in their bedrooms and we see our college friends honeymooning in far off places, but that's not what marriage was designed for.

As a woman who desires to love well, we know, in the depths of our hearts, that those things do not mark a good marriage. We've seen clearly that many marriages were built as vacation getaways, not as foundational homesteads. Trust me, time always tells. Everyone starts out in love and happy, but the end is always more telling than the beginning. The ending points to the work, whereas the beginnings are comprised of the daydream. It's why there are approximately 6,500 divorces being finalized in America each week[6]. That's 6,500 marriages who exchanged rings and kisses, vacations and physical pleasures in the beginning, but it wasn't enough to endure. Marriage, God's way, was designed to last, because it was curated by God to inhabit and exhibit spiritual treasures, rather than mere earthly ones. Worldly ambitions aren't enough to produce lasting love or even lasting emotions. These things are temporary, therefore the result from pursuing them are temporary, as well. Décor is not enough. God's design entails more, and therefore will produce more. If a godly marriage is what you desire, only a strong

---

[6] U.S. Marriage and Divorce Rates by State. Retrieved January 10, 2020, https://www.census.gov

foundation of Christ's unshakable love will make your love unshakable. What I'm talking about reaches further than routinely going to church or affirming a Christian belief system. Even within homes that profess Christianity, 33% experience divorce [7]. So, what's the deal? Professing the religion of Christianity will not keep your life free from divorce. Rather a lifestyle which practices the principles of worship by investing in a relationship with Christ makes the difference. His love teaches us to love in eternal ways. Our feelings are real experiences, but they don't last, and they seldom occur the way we expect them to. This isn't wrong, it's factual, so basing love off of feelings is impractical. Rings won't change hearts. Only Christ's love can do that. It has nothing to do with emotions, but everything to do with the divine mission of the Gospel within our marriages and in our lives.

Loving When You're Low

As we pursue the Lord in our lives and in our marriages, sometimes, the growth that His love demands will put us in vulnerable positions where we have to choose to love when we don't want to or when it feels impossible to do so. But God's

---

[7] New Marriage and Divorce Statistics Released. (n.d.). Retrieved January 10, 2020, from https://www.barna.com/research/new-marriage-and-divorce-statistics-released/

design of covenant love empowers us to make the choice to love each other, even in the moments when you struggle to like each other. All marriages go through rough times. The Obamas have gone through rough times in their marriage. Your pastors have gone through rough times, too. Your parents, your siblings, your best friends, the social media influencers, Basketball Wives … every marriage has its highs and its lows. And some lows can get really low. It's a dangerous belief system that equates good marriages with good emotions. If, according to our society, happy feelings are the basis for which we deem a marriage's worth, then every single marriage should end in divorce. What a scary thought.

Five years ago, I almost lost my life in childbirth. It was a terrifying experience that created awful memories which sometimes still wake me up at night. Death is very, very silent and bitterly cold and I know its presence well. It was a still summer night without any indication that it would change my life. We were three weeks away from our due date and Jarrett and I went to bed like any other evening. Many of the details are such a blur, but I remember my husband carrying me to the car, my blood on his hands and worry all over his face. There was no way of knowing exactly how much I hemorrhaged before arriving at the hospital, but the doctors estimated that I lost 1.2 liters of blood in their custody. I couldn't feel any of the intense spikes of contractions that the monitors were showing because I kept slipping in and out of consciousness. My body was going into shock. I couldn't focus, I couldn't think, and I couldn't even pray, but the waiting room was filled with family who were fervently covering me and Kailyn. There was no threat on her life, but mine hung in the balance. Two blood transfusions, drugs and a surgery later, I came home feeling hallow. I didn't want Jarrett at all, and I didn't want him seeing me so weak. My new scar disgusted me, and my recovery process drained me. I wasn't allowed to do much and though Jarrett was so loving and so present, I struggled tremendously. That was the lowest point in our marriage, thus far. We smiled in public a lot, but there were so many muted moments between us behind closed doors. Our daughter's crying filled the room where laughter used to be and though he'd reach for my hand, I didn't have much strength to give him my heart. I was intimately incompetent. I was in a lot of pain, physically, while trying to heal, mentally. Yet every night, Jarrett prayed over me, out loud, and I watched my husband do all he could to support me. I'd wake up to kisses and breakfast and cards singed, "Love, Jarrett". We went to church, watched our baby grow and sought council. I read Proverbs 31 over and over again, as well as Song of Songs and 1 Corinthians 13. I prayed for my life to come back. I was tired of faking in front of my friends. I was tired of smiling for the pictures. I wanted to feel again. I wanted to come back to life.

Those first few months of my new motherhood produced some very low times in our marriage. I loved being a mother and caring for our child, but it was the intimate part of my marriage that was placed on pause because I was terrified of getting pregnant again – afraid I wouldn't survive a second labor. It was a pain I never knew existed – anxiety, uncertainty. Jarrett wanted to help me, but I felt so helpless. I wanted his understanding, but he couldn't comprehend what I was unable to express. There were days when I wanted to refuse everything my husband offered because I just didn't feel worthy of it and I knew he was feeling quite rejected.

Talking to my Mother one day, I realized that when I use my feelings as an excuse to refuse Jarrett's loving efforts, I was being unloving. God's design for marriage is to reach past the pain and the hell and the grave. His love is life giving and it reaches far into the depths of us the moment we invite Him in. This is what Jarrett needed from me. He needed to be invited in. He needed me to let him hold me, even though I didn't feel emotionally intimate. He needed me to let him help with our daughter. He needed me to love him with the love of Jesus Christ. I needed this, too. So, I gave my fear to Jesus and, in small ways, began to reach for my husband again.

That conversation with my Mother lead me to embrace the truth that I needed to allow my husband to love me and I needed to stop pushing him away based on my inconsistent feelings. Even though I had such strong fear and lack of emotions towards intimacy, entrusting these things to the Lord placed our marriage back on a healthy trajectory. With time, I started reciprocating; first in little ways, then in more intimate ways. It was a choice I had to ask the Lord to help me make. I could continue to sink deeper into my feelings (both the physical and the emotional feelings), or I could actively love my husband by allowing the unconditional love of Jesus to heal my anxieties through scripture and prayer. I didn't always want to, but prayer helped me realize that loving Jarrett was more important than my feelings and that healing was only possible through Jesus.

It's in this ugly season where I deeply grasped and learned the truth that love is not a feeling. Love is a choice and it's a virtue and in order to love unconditionally, in spite of myself and in spite of outside situations or people, it requires a relationship with Jesus, as declared in the Gospel. Healing, restoration, new beginnings and transformations are a promise for our lives, no matter how high or how low our stories take us. Through this problem in our marriage, and in my personal life, we saw how giving and receiving the love of God for one another renewed us and sustained us. It wasn't always easy. There were so many tears and nightmares and conversations and baby steps away from the grips of fear and back into the loving arms of courage and intimacy, but when I look back, I see how that situation grew our roots deeper in love and in covenant – past the feelings and beyond the emotions. Those things have absolutely nothing to do with loving well.

Two years later, we birthed a second baby girl and I cannot begin to express the joy our daughters have filled our lives with! Kailyn and Jaelle are our treasures and my personal miracles! My motherhood is miraculous and it's all because of the Lord and because of my husband. The love of Christ in Jarrett reached down deep to touch me in places that felt dead. It may not sound like much of a love story but it is; it's part of my love story with Jarrett and with Jesus.

A Divine Challenge

There are so many reasons why people decide to get married, but I want to ask you: are the reasons you decided to get married the same reasons why you have decided to stay married? If yes, that's a wonderful security you have; if no, you are the most honest person in the room! It's ok. It's difficult to make decisions regarding situations we've never gone through before and sometimes, we have to stop and reevaluate our motives (1 Timothy 1:5) in order to cultivate what our hearts truly yearn for. That was my battle– I had to be honest enough to admit that I needed to reevaluate what love was and revisit God's design for marriage. It's this reevaluation that lead me in prayer because conviction showed me that my feelings had gotten in the way of my loving.

I challenge you to courageously evaluate your own motives for loving. Is it for yourself? Is it for your family or is it for Jesus? Listen, all other ground is sinking sand. To love another person because of how they make you feel will not secure either one of you. But love, according to the Bible, is about filling the other person's heart. It's a covenant, which was designed by God, to empty ourselves of our self-interests so that we can pour into one another and fulfill the mission of loving like Jesus.

"Do nothing from selfish ambition or self-interest, but in humility count others more significant than yourselves. Let each of you look not only to his own interests, but also to the interests of others. Have this mind among yourselves, which is yours in Christ Jesus"
-Philippians 2:4-5 (ESV).

God's way of loving and His design for marriage has always been about reaching past ourselves and pouring our love into the other person, come what may. It's not always pretty, but it sure is beautiful! A woman who desires to love well will love well, even when loving is a challenge. The success of your marriage is not in your feelings. Don't believe those lies, because they are dangerous and deceptive. Our feelings are always changing, irrational and unpredictable. There are no guarantees in life, but one thing is sure: the love of Christ never fails (1 Corinthians 3:8). His love is active and true and dependable and secure, especially when ours is unable to be. The truth is that we have to choose this love and then choose to extend it in our marriages and also with the world around us. In this way, we can share the love of Christ, which is pure and simple, steadfast and eternal. No one can fulfill another person completely, except the Lord. It's His love that compels us to keep loving, even when our emotions tell us it's impossible. The challenge is never in the doing, but rather in the believing and obeying. As the Gospel grows in us, through a relationship with Jesus, we see how His love never fails and therefore a marriage centered in Him will not fail, either. No matter the feelings, the season or the challenges, we can love in the light of the Gospel and make the daily decision to be women who love well, even when we're not feeling it.

Reflection

75

How does knowing God's design for marriage impact the way you love your husband?

<u>Scriptures for Your Soul</u>

"And walk in love, as Christ loved us and gave himself up for us, a fragrant offering and sacrifice to God."
-Ephesians 5:2

"Therefore, a man shall leave his father and mother and hold fast to his wife, and the two shall become one flesh." This mystery is profound, and I am saying that it refers to Christ and the church."
-Ephesians 5:31-32 (ESV)

76

CHAPTER 3

THE RIGHT ONE

"Do you ever wonder if Jarrett is the right one for you?"

My sweet friend asked me this question a few years back. She was having some doubts at the time and needed some encouragement; it was one of the rawest and most vulnerable conversations she and I had ever had. As I listened, my eyes began to burn and water while she confessed resentment and fear and lost hope in her marriage. An unexpected move had taken her completely out of her comfort zone and miles from everything that felt secure. It was one of those life changes that just wasn't in her plans.

"Nothing will ever be the same again", she told me. "He should just quit and find another job so that we can go back home. I hate it here. I told him not to take this job", she said. "My life would be so much better if …"

I could hear the pain in her crackling voice. I knew she was going through a very real personal storm. She had doubts about her husband and doubts about her current season in life. All this caused her so much worry and worry created anxieties that lead her down a path of "what if". It's a place many of us go to from time to time in our minds. Our doubts lead us to picture a life that isn't real and place us in situations that have only occurred in our minds. Dwelling on these things for too long can begin to take a toll on the life that we are actually living. It can take our problems and project them onto our marriages, distracting us from the blessings all around us. How many of us have experienced this? How many of us have found ourselves contemplating doubts regarding our lives and our marriages? If we aren't careful, it can cause us to question if our spouse was the right choice.

Disconnecting from Doubt

When we say, "I do", we have no idea what we are pledging ourselves to. As we discussed in the previous chapter, those vows we make are heavy promises and we have no control over what those promises will demand from us. Does sickness mean the flu or cancer? Does poor mean a missed light bill or homelessness? Of course, we consider that hard times could come, but in what ways? We don't know. We aren't privy to such knowledge and neither are our husbands. Doubt screams, "mistake", when we experience discomfort or disappointment. But women who desire to love well do so through the problems and the pain and the pressure. Love covers all (1 Peter 4:8), but it doesn't prevent all things. We will absolutely experience distresses in life, but love can be an anchor through it all when you secure one another safely in the hope that love brings.

Listening to my friend's vulnerable honesty broke my heart and I wanted so badly to tell her that things would all work out and that her husband's stress at work would subside and he would be more present with her; that their finances would improve so that perhaps they could come home more often, and she could see her mom and her friends more regularly and not feel so alone. I wanted to say all those things, but who was I to promise this?

The truth is, none of us know what lies ahead, but these unknowns are critical in shaping our lives and our hearts. They don't have to be given the power to ruin our marriages. Good, loving and strong marriages are secured in the promises we've made by entrusting those promises to the Lord. Love is His promise and your marriage is His work. These are the truths I am learning to hold onto in order to encourage my heart because my marriage, and yours, has so many wonderous things to be encouraged by! We've been blessed to love another person as fully and as deeply as we decide to! What an honor and a privilege we should never lose sight of!

I have no idea where you are currently in your marriage, but I want you to rejoice alongside you for all the loveliness that your marriage has the potential to produce! Disconnecting from our doubts positions us to better keep insight the blessings in our marriages, currently and the promises for our marriages yet to come. Remember, we are supposed to think on things above!

"Since then, you have been raised with Christ, set your hearts on things above, where Christ is, seated at the right hand of God. Set your minds on things above, not on earthly things."
-Colossians 3: 1-2 (NIV)

Thinking on things above means we aren't dwelling on doubt. Doubt always points out the negatives. Doubt always questions our choices and doubt will cause you to question your marriage. Don't give doubt your ear or space in your thought life anymore. Instead, think on what is lovely and good and true and pure and worthy about your marriage (Philippians 4:8). It takes hope and prayer, but we have the victory to control our thought life by casting down vain imaginations as declared in 2 Corinthians 10:5. What this means is that we do not have to invest time in dwelling on negative situations or scenarios that haven't occurred yet. Anxiety is the worry of problems that might happen, while distracting us from appreciating the blessings that are currently happening. I'd rather dwell on what God is doing, rather than doubt what He may or may not do. So, I want to remind you that there are for sure good things that are occurring in your marriage right now. Love is happening! Always. All the time. It's happening every time you open your Bible. It's happening every time you share a smile with your husband. Love is happening every time you experience the new morning mercies of God and it's happening every time you choose obedience (John 14:15). You are never without love and you are never too far removed from the opportunity to love your husband well. No matter what it looks like, what it feels like or what it's perceived to be like, there are treasures just waiting to be celebrated in your marriage when you begin distance yourself from doubt, because doubt will distance your heart from loving the one that is right in front of you.

<u>Prayer Paves the Way</u>

Doubt is always accompanied by worry and anxiety and neither point us to prayer. It's notable that, when life is good and going well, we're so confident in our love, but when life feels out of control, we doubt the exact same person. That's what doubt does. It distracts us and deceives us. It causes us to look at the storm instead of our Savior (Matthew 14: 22-33). Like crashing waves, doubt drives our hearts to worry about what we cannot predict or control, rather than petitioning our Heavenly Father for His direction and guidance in our circumstances. Prayer, not worry, is what will pave our way through the storms of life and marriage. If Christ is our anchor, then He will not let us go.

What I am learning is that prayer is an open invitation to remind my heart that Jesus is in control! My marriage is part of His plan for me, therefore my husband is the right one for me. When I pray, it builds my trust and as I trust, I am more thankful and less doubtful. Have you ever noticed this in your life? Prayer pulls us closer to God when we seek His will and not our own because prayer isn't about getting our anticipated answer from God, it's about simply drawing near to Him as He makes His answers clear to us. There are many false teachings out there that tell us that prayer is a conduit to ensure we get what we want from God, but I want to remind us that God's plans, His thoughts and His ways are so much greater than ours could ever be (Isaiah 55:8). Prayer, therefore, isn't a tool to convince God to give us what we want, but it's an opportunity that God extends to us to show us that He is all we need. When we pray, we should have humble hearts to hear from God and to receive whatever it is that He has for us, for our marriage and for our family, because He has promised that all His plans for us are good (Jeremiah 29:11).

Prayer invites God's presence and His presence gives us peace, so, as we pray for direction, discernment and understanding, God's presence reveals His blessings which are already occurring in our marriages. This begins to position us into praise and thanksgiving, rather than anxiety, doubt or worry. We can then transform our thoughts from complaining into celebrating as we thank the Lord for our husband's growth, his efforts, his friendship and his love. This not only sets the mood in our homes, but also in our hearts because God's presence is always found in our praise (Matthew 18:20).

This was the conversation my friend and I began to discuss over the phone. We began to revisit God's promises that He will never leave us or forsake us (Hebrews 13:5) and that He always has good plans for us (Jeremiah 29:11) and that it's He who orders our steps (Psalm 37:23). We prayed over her marriage and thanked the Lord for her husband's devotion to his family, his work ethic and his determination. We praised God for her future and for how far she's come as a person, as a professional, as a wife and as a child of God. Without a doubt, the atmosphere began to change as our prayers and our thoughts pressed more into God's promises rather than the problems! I think we both heaved a sigh of relief as she ditched the doubt to think on things above!

I wish our lives could always be filled with champagne nights and fireworks, but I am learning that it's the problems that produce powerful testimonies and a deeper focus on the Lord and on our marriages. Prayer propels us to think on things above. These are the things that we soar on, even when the wind tries to knock us down. God is faithful to comfort us when we call on Him in prayer (2 Corinthians 1:3). All things are purposed for His glory and His Gospel and we can rely on His promises as we go through difficult seasons because God's love never fails. Never. He is a promise keeper, even in times when it feels we are unable to keep the promises we've made. Prayer is essential to combat the clouds of doubt. God's love and His wisdom is ushered in through prayer to shift our perspective and realign our hearts in every situation: good and bad, desperate and delight.

An Everyday Decision

Without fail, every morning, my day begins with Jarrett pushing back my hair and kissing me. Rain or shine, late or timely, sick, tired ... he does this without fail. Jarrett is always showing me Jesus in this way. God has given me such grace through my husband and his commitment to love me and intentionally choose me, in spite of my moods. He's always showing me that he loves me with his life and not just with his words. His passion and daily pursuit of me beacons me to dive deeper in our marriage and allures my heart to grow in more grace to choose him daily, as well.

Though I am so undeserving, God is teaching me that loving my husband is a daily gift that He grants me as an example of how His unconditional love chooses me each and every day. Intimately, like a lover's kiss, God invites us to invite His love into our hearts and into our homes. Our decision to respond to this invitation empowers us to extend the same grace to our spouses, no matter how the day began or ended. Not every night is a good one, but every morning can be! It all depends on your decision to choose love and to choose your spouse over and over again because your life will never be the novel. It will never be the daydream; I believe it can become better than that! It begins with a resolve to love every day, just as the Lord loves us.

The longer I am married, the more firmly I believe that our husbands are our gifts. They are not our benefactors and we are not their trophies. We are sacred treasures, therefore we must handle each other as such, deciding, no matter what, to meet each other's needs in the sacred mission of marriage on a daily basis. I am absolutely convinced that loving well is a choice. We were the ones who chose our husbands, after all, we said, "yes", stuck out our hand and accepted his ring. We chose to repeat the vows and kiss our groom. We willingly signed the papers and changed our names. These were decisions that we made, and this was a part of God's plan for our good and for His glory!

Because we know that every plan of God includes a hope and a future (Jeremiah 29:11), we know that we can trust the Lord and trust the love that He has placed in our lives. I realize this is so simple to read but complicated to live out sometimes and choosing our husbands every day isn't always easy and can occasionally feel like a task we'd rather put on the shelf. But, as my Mother use to tell me, "good things don't come easy, sweet girl". I want to say the same to you and challenge you to always invest in your good things!

John 15:13 tells us, "Greater love has no man than this, that he lay down his life for his friends." Considering this as an instruction for marriage, understand that choosing our marriage requires us to lay down our lives, our self-interests, comfort zones and personal agendas in order to love our husbands more highly than we love ourselves (Philippians 2:3). This is submission and it's what pleases God. On the surface, it might seem like a forfeit of personal freedom, rights, and, to any modern feminist, demeaning, but understand that submission is a command for both a husband and a wife.

Ephesians 5:21 tells us to submit to one another as in reverence to Christ. Consider how fulfilling our marriages would be if we both made the daily decision to choose one another by treating each other as more important than ourselves; laying aside both of our selfishness for one another and choosing to live our lives in total service to one another's hearts. Imagine the impacts that would make on our conversations, on our spending habits, on our sex lives and in our emotional health. Laying down our lives sounds terrifying, but when we each make this choice (just as Christ has made for us) we find that it is truly a beautiful decision with resounding results and unrelenting abundance.

The daily decision to choose our husband and put him first isn't easy. What is easy is requiring to be served first, to be catered to and to be accommodated. Demanding the apology is easy. Giving the silent treatment or yelling out belittling words is easy. Using manipulative means to get our way … that's easy. These decisions are selfish and won't produce better love because "easy" is quick and short lived. It won't produce growth or substance in our marriage or in our lives. It might seem strong and passionate in the movies, but choosing ourselves is the easy thing to do and will corrode our marriages from the inside-out. As the Bible tells us, those who choose to cling to their lives will end up losing it, but the ones who choose to give their lives will win them in the end (Matthew 10:39).

Does any of this make you feel uncomfortable? It's ok if it does. I know it goes against everything our culture tells us about being respected and being strong. I pray that the Lord will renew our minds from the deception that has taken a toll on our generation when it comes to self-value and self-love. Please don't believe the lie that self-love is of more importance than God's love. I know this is a popular line in our movies, novels and songs, but loving well requires us to place our selfishness into submission, every day, so that the selfless love of God can shine through. It's not easy. Sometimes, it's very difficult, but as I've said in my previous book, so I say it again because it applies: God did not call us to be easy women. He called us to be lights in a dark world and fragrances of hope to impact others for the Kingdom (2 Corinthians 2:15).

I want to encourage you that weather you're having a difficult time making financial decisions or struggling to cool off from a small disagreement, you are a strong woman and strong women aren't afraid of difficult things. Strong women step out into the water and intentionally walk towards greater. Strong women see the giants and run towards them. Strong women see the flames and know that they will not consume her. How is this possible? It's because the presence of God brings peace, comfort and courage. Strong women know they are not alone, and they know they are living for more than just themselves. Let the Lord fuel your daily decisions to choose to love well and to love right. Trust that God's love within you has equipped you to make the daily decision to do the greatest thing: to love God with all your heart, mind, soul and strength, and to love your neighbor as yourself. Your husband is your neighbor and he needs the strength of your love, just as you need his.

The daily decision to choose our spouse won't always be easy, yet it's the difficult things which produce greatness and cultivate character. Remember always that love chooses to receive when rejection is so much easier. Love enables us to choose grace rather than render punishment; forgiveness, rather than vindication; compassion, instead of condemnation. Love gives the kisses, even when we're pissed. Love goes to work even when we are tired. Love cooks the food, even when we feel unappreciated. Love extends itself, even when we feel offended or disrespected and love builds the other up, even when we feel drained or unnoticed.

Loving God's way isn't easy, but it is full of true joy! As we trust Him to lead us into loving our right ones the right way, our marriages will grow in confidence to do whatever is necessary in protecting the love we are intentionally cultivating. This requires us to say what needs to be said and do what needs to be done in order to maintain harmony, health and healing. A woman who desires to love well is not going to play games when it comes to her marriage. Just reach for him. In so doing, you will uplift your marriage as well as your man. He wants to be chosen, too! He wants to feel needed and missed and thought of, too! It starts with the simple everyday gestures of intentionality.

Every day, I wear Jarrett's ring. Every day, I say, "yes", to him. I keep a journal full of compliments I plan to say to him for the next day and I look for ways to lift him up simply because he's mine. When it's necessary, I will address my concerns and annoyances with him, but never to tear him down. I try very hard to express how much I love him and then I support what I say by living out my love in meaningful ways that he appreciates. When I've done wrong, I'm open to hearing his concerns and if I don't agree, I'm open to being corrected. I apologize when necessary and I pray constantly. These have been my decisions on how I go about actively loving and supporting my husband. Explore some things you can start implementing in your marriage!

Remember, decisions take intentionality to implement. The mindset, "Let's just see where it goes", may have been your style in dating, but it isn't conducive for marriage. I want every wife to realize the power of her choice within her marriage and I want every wife to know that God is working in you and through you and that your marriage is purposed. Even in the difficulties, the Lord uses your marriage to meet a need in your life. It's your decision whether or not to celebrate that.

I know you desire to choose the loving thing and I am cheering you on to continue in your pursuits because your husband needs to see that you are choosing him, every day. He needs to see that you have made the decision to reach for him and champion him. He needs to see that you are excited to kiss him and be touched by him. He needs to hear you complementing him on a job well done. He needs to be shown genuine affection, not routine toleration. I know you want to. I know you're trying. I'm here to celebrate you and encourage you to never stop.

<u>Living Out Love</u>

This marriage that you are in, or are about to enter into, is sacred and it's providential. It's not random and it's not a mistake. Compatibility is desirable, but no one is compatible with another person in everything or in every way. You're going to have some differences and those differences can produce disappointment, or they can produce opportunities for enhanced living and loving. Marriage does have a way of magnifying our flaws, but maybe that's the point. Maybe unity and compatibility aren't natural occurrences, but they can be achieved through living out our love, intentionally and unconditionally. We've got to realize that loving our husband in our comfort zone is not enough. We must recognize the need to open our hearts to live out the love that we so desire to enjoy in our marriage. A woman who desires to love well understands this. She resolves to operate beyond contingencies and ultimatums. Her life is committed in service to her family, first, and she pushes herself beyond trifle appearances and rudimentary comforts. She knows that her husband is worth her devotion and that God is truly working in the details of their marriage.

God is near. Always.

He's always one prayer away, one page away, one breath away. He knows everything you think and feel, and He hears every word you speak. He knew that you desired marriage. He knew that you desired more than Friday nights in crowded places. He positioned you to be at the right place at the right time for a miraculous meeting and introductions. He placed an interest in your man to notice you and pursue you. Your husband is God's best for you because God aligned your hearts to birth the desire to marry one another. This is God's work and sometimes, He uses the difficult things to intertwine and refine two imperfect people into one beautiful example of His unconditional and infinite love.

The Gospel beacons us to live out our love by intentionally giving our hearts to our husbands, as unto the Lord. Such purposed choices produce major flames and those flames create some good love'n! There is freedom in God's love and with so many failed marriages and broken homes in our society, I do not want any of us to come out defeated. I want all of us to grow deeper in love with our husbands, gaining rich and nourishing lessons along the way. What we go through is not who we are, but who we are will be visible in what we go through.

When harmony is threatened by the differences between us, how will we respond? Will we give up, declare we're done and walk away? Or will we rise to be the valiant women we've been called to be, encourage our men to be the gallant men they've been called to be and run on mission to love one another like Jesus? That's the question. That's the choice, because unconditional love is just that - love without condition. My prayer is that we all choose to love without limits and to pray for a greater grace to love like Christ because His love is the anchor and the answer for every doubt and every season as you continue in your pursuits to love well and to love right.

<u>Loving Right</u>

When we married our husband, he became the "right one". Yes, I am talking about your man! You chose each other, therefore he is right for you. Regardless of the hard times or the good times, he is the right one because a covenant was made with him in the presence of God. Those are the only requirements for our husbands to become our "Mr. Right".

"What God has joined together, let no man put asunder."
-Mark 10:9 (KJV)

God wants to show your husband His unconditional love through the ways that you love your husband, unconditionally. How powerful is that?! How beautiful and deep and heavy and lovely! Everything that touches our lives, God will use it. It's not a waste. Your joys, confusion, excitements and disappointments are not proof of whether or not you chose wrong; they're all opportunities to love right!

What I love most about my husband is how willing he is to offer me his love. I must admit that it's not always so easy for me. I've been guilty of shutting down completely or walking out of the room during moments of conflict. I slam doors sometimes and demand "alone time" when I'm frustrated. Though I know I am not perfect, I must confess that what I perceive to be flaws in Jarrett sometimes disappoint me, and I've regrettably reacted in unbecoming ways. It's human nature, but when our spouse's flaws clash with us, it can cause many women, and men, to second guess their compatibility with their spouse and their commitment all together. At some point, we may all find ourselves thinking, "He's not the person I thought he was". At some point, he may think the exact same thing about you. It's normal. You're not wrong, you're human.

But loving well and loving right isn't about fixing what we consider to be problems in one another. We can sit high on our pride and try to fix our husbands, and everyone else around us for that matter, but love doesn't look down on others; it always looks up! The Bible says that love rejoices in the truth (1 Corinthians 13:6). I am learning that this means that I must switch my perspective and celebrate the strengths of my husband, rather than dwelling on what I wish would change. Whatever concerns me, I give it to God in prayer; whatever astounds me, I speak life over it and use my opportunities to encourage him to reach higher and run faster.

Dormant flaws and unsuspecting weaknesses have a way of waking up within our marriages, but rarely beforehand. It's why my Father is adamant that no one truly knows their spouse until a few years after the marriage has taken place. In covenant, things are revealed and in the midst of the unveiling, we begin to see one another for who we truly are. This should bring us to our knees in thankfulness for the Lord's graciousness in our lives. Listen, none of us are perfect and none of us deserve love. It's not something we are owed and it's nothing that someone is obligated to give us. It's a gift and the right response is always to receive it and then offer it back.

You may feel tempted to wonder, at times, if you made the right choice. You're not a bad person for these doubts. It is perfectly normal because we have no idea what other paths may have been available to us outside of the choices we made. But please listen to me well when I say that God is ordering your steps and your every decision was already pre-recorded (Proverbs 16:9). Your desire to love your husband is precious and it's purposed and though it may not be a fairy tale, it is a treasure for each of you to enjoy in the fullness and abundance of one another's love. There is no mistake in that. Love isn't about the "right one", it's about loving the one you chose in the right way – God's way – no matter the struggles, weaknesses or difficulties that you cannot control.

I must be sure to insert, however, the issues of domestic abuse and violence, which also includes verbal abuse, are not the imperfections and flaws that I'm referring to. Abuse is oppression and it's another thing that God hates.

"What do you mean by crushing my people, by grinding the face of the poor?"
declares the Lord God of hosts. -Isaiah 3: 15 (ESV)

Abuse is a horrific sin. It's selfish, faithless and a horrendous failure in loving like Christ (Ephesians 5:25). I firmly believe that anyone who desires to conduct themselves and their marriage with God's love will have a tender heart of compassion and concern, not a heart of violence or punishment. They would be adamant about pleasing the Lord and pleasing their spouse, because where the Spirit of the Lord is, there is liberty (2 Corinthians 3:17).

If you find yourself, or someone you know, in an abusive situation, please get help. It's not your fault and it's not your failure. It's sin and it's a crime, in God's eyes as well as in the law of our land. God's way of loving is uplifting, not demeaning. No one is perfect, but again, Salvation in Christ ignites our hearts with the power of perfect love because the love of Christ is perfect. Yes, we will make mistakes. This is true. But mistakes are not habitual. They are not a part of our lifestyle. Abuse is not a mistake. It's not a mere flaw. It is an abominable choice and void of every fruit of the Spirit: love, joy, peace, patients, kindness, goodness, faithfulness, gentleness, and self-control (Galatians 5:22-23).

These fruits are evident in our marriage when we love the right way. This is God's way of loving us, therefore, it's how we should love and be loved by one other. It's possible, even in the difficulties, because this perfect love for our imperfect hearts is always available to us through Jesus. His gifts never run dry, so we can take courage and confidence in knowing that the husbands we chose are, indeed, right for us, and we can love them well with the perfect love of Jesus!

No matter how perfect your relationship seems to be, or you hope it to be, problems are a part of the packaged deal. How we deal with our problems and how we respond to our spouses says more about our love than romance or happy days ever could. Every storm seems devastating, but the lightning and rain make things greener, stronger and grow with greater abundance.

I want to encourage you that if God put you together, then your husband is the right one for you. Understand that your marriage is not at fault for the storms that may swirl around you. Storms will come whether you are married or not, but every disappointment is seasonal. They don't last forever and the lessons and growth that can be cultivated because of those disappointments can certainly bolster our love and enhance our unions.

The question of the "right one", is a tempting doubt to entertain, especially when there is conflict –the one without problems, the one who is predictable and comfortable and safe, is he still out there? Did I miss him? My answer is simply, "no, you didn't", because a man like that doesn't exist. That man and that marriage isn't real, but the man you chose to marry is. He is real and he is filled with real love for you! Once we resolve to love one another through the difficult unknowns, rather than allow disappointments to create long term indifference, despair or doubt, we will soon find that the "right one" is actually the one whom God entrusted us to be with all along.

Reflection

What are some practical ways you show your husband that he is your "Right One"?

<u>Scriptures for Your Soul</u>

"Steadfast love and faithfulness meet; righteousness and peace kiss each other."
-Psalm 85:10 (NIV)

"And we know that for those who love God all things work together for good, for those who are called according to His purpose."
-Romans 8:28 (NLT)

CHAPTER 4

CULTIVATING COMMUNICATION

One of my favorite things to do is talk. When I feel comfortable, I'll talk to anyone about anything. And when I'm not talking, I'm writing because words are very important to me. The ability to express myself, to give my opinion, encourage a friend, write a book ... all those things require my words and I enjoy engaging others in this way. But marriage has shown me, in some very humbling occasions, that being a confident talker is not the same as being an effective communicator. My husband has definitely challenged me by showing me a time or two where I can be more interested in my own words than in hearing his.

What I am constantly learning is that strong communication isn't necessary for conflicts only. It's important in maintaining connectivity with one another through every area, moment and experience. Healthy people in healthy relationships desire to stay in touch with one another for conversation, interest, play, affirmation and affection. Each of these moments begins with conversation. When we take intentional turns to talk and listen, we create opportunities to connect, understand and implement the needs of both people in the marriage. You've no doubt heard this, read this and may have had dozens of conversations on the topic of communication within your lifetime. Sometimes, over exposure to a familiar fact can cause us to forget the need to implement it, but I urge us all to take some serious inventory regarding our conversations within our marriages, seek ways to improve it and evaluate habits that inhibit loving and productive conversations.

No matter who we are or how long we've been married, we should aspire to grow more in our communication methods with our husbands in intentional and authentic ways. It's one of the fundamental means we connect on matters that help us grow as women, as well as wives. Discussing and listening go hand and hand, as does our body language and nonverbal messages. It takes honesty, some serious self-evaluation and personal awareness to decipher if our true bent lies in an open understanding of one another or merely in getting our point across. I'll admit that I have to check myself often when it comes to the "listening verses hearing" aspect of communication. Coming from a very opinionated family, it's taken me a while to grasp the notion that, though my words and opinions are important, Jarrett's words are equally valuable and listening to him not only gives him a chance to be heard, it also provides me the opportunity to decisively discover who he is and who he is becoming. Healthy communication ultimately desires connection. People who love want to pour themselves out to one another because in doing so, we discover each other and we grow closer to one another. We can learn about our inner most thoughts and secret parts and we can explore the heart of our lover – a place where no one else has the invitation to investigate. When you look at it this way, communication and conversation can be a wonderful thing, rather than a scary thing because discussions shouldn't merely be a means reserved for disagreements or conflicts only. Just think back to when you were dating! How many nights did you spend just talking about whatever popped up in your head? School, work, family, futures, stress, friendships, goals, failures, fears, intimacy, spirituality ... none of those initial conversations were had because of conflict. You both opened up your lives to one another because you were interested in getting to know each other in authentic and meaningful ways and the adventure of falling in love gave you the courage to risk exposing and expressing yourselves as a means to grow deeper in your relationship. This is what honesty and healthy conversations look like! It's beautiful and it's something we all did during dating. It shouldn't stop after marriage.

An Ongoing Discovery

According to Dr. Les and Leslie Parrott, award winning Christian Marriage counselors who have successfully supported millions of marriages, love relationships maintain themselves linguistically throughout its duration. In their book, *Love Talk*, they make this profound statement, "weather a relationship sinks or swims depends on how well couples send and receive messages, and how well they use their conversations to understand and be understood."[8] Wow! Think about that: understand and understood.

When your conversations never go deeper than routine words, when you don't spend time talking about what lies below the surface of your individual lives, a sense of loneliness and unfamiliarity between a husband and wife can begin to merge and eventually, the very essence of the relationship can begin to feel abandoned or attacked. So often, many couples begin to feel that the distance and space between their words are, in actuality, an expression of the separation between their lives. But it's nothing that a meaningful conversation can't improve. We have to be willing to say the things we are secretively thinking and feeling because those things are vital for the wellbeing of our relationships. Our words are windows into our hearts and our conversations guide us into learning one another through ongoing and loving discoveries.

A wife who desires to love well wants to improve her communication in order to support the health and growth of her marriage. Good communication makes everyone feel valued and it keeps our marriages current. The lack of it could create long term emotional damage and I believe that we have to be careful not to

---

[8] Parrott, L., & Parrott, L. L. (2019). *Love Talk: Speak Each Other's Language Like You Never Have Before*. Grand Rapids, MI: Zondervan.

allow our thoughts, fears or assumptions deafen the words that are being spoken to us or that need to be spoken by us.

Our communication is crucial to a sustaining and fulfilling marriage, yet many of us struggle to communicate effectively, and therefore decide not to communicate at all. Instead, we use other means to avoid awkward or uncertain discussions. Sex gets used as a tool to escape the risk of digging deeper. Kids and other outside relationships can also be an excuse used to avoid intimate conversations. So often, healthy communication in marriage is often not taken seriously enough until we are desperate and in need to understand and be understood.

Friends, we don't have to wait until we are desperate. We can begin building habits of healthy conversations now and train our hearts and ears to enjoy the verbal discovery that will lead us beyond our words and into our love. Communication is the conduit through which all other vital aspects of thriving relationships are achieved. Let's embrace it and learn to cultivate it for the benefit and prosperity of our marriages.

Disconnect to Reconnect

When Jarrett and I take a drive, I sit in the passenger seat and ramble on and on. I sing out loud and I talk about my day, my friends, my clients, my questions … whatever. But, Jarret doesn't talk much at all. He just holds my hand and comments here and there. He laughs at my jokes and he answers my questions, but he's never been one to philosophise. He much prefers to contemplate his own thoughts before sharing them. Since it's so easy for me to express my every-teeny-tiny thought or idea, I naturally want him to be just as comfortable. For me, talking is an outlet, but for Jarrett, thinking is an outlet. He doesn't need to spill his guts on a daily basis in order to make sense of his world. He doesn't need to know what I had for lunch or how many minutes I was late to work. It's not that imperative for him to ask me if I talked to my mom about her new plant or her recent shopping trip. He'd rather ponder his day and his thoughts and open up once he's come to a conclusion he'd like to discuss with me; whereas I like to discuss everything with him in order to arrive at a conclusion. Yeah, opposites attract for us, but I've realized that the differences in how we connect balance us out.

During our first years of marriage, there were nights when I went to bed frustrated because I felt like we hadn't connected deeply that day. Like a lot of guys, Jarrett isn't moved to say a lot of words and prefers connecting through shoulder-to-shoulder time more so than gibber-jabber. If you're unfamiliar with that term, let me explain. Shoulder-to-shoulder time is time spent doing activities or watching activities without much dialogue, if any. A lot of men don't need to talk. Many prefer to experience their world through their senses, as opposed to how some women enjoy experiencing their world through engagement. [9] So basically, some husbands are happy as long as they can see you, touch you, and smell you. That's a good

---

[9] Eggerichs, E. (2010). *Love and Respect: The Love She Most Desires, The Respect He Desperately Needs*. Detroit: Thomas Nelson Publishing.

day for him! Women, on the other hand, tend to need more engaging connection. We want eye contact, we want to ask and answer questions, we want to "feel connected" through an exchange of thoughts, whether that be during an activity or during a conversation.

It's a no brainer that men and women have different ways of connecting. Neither is right or wrong and of course, there are always exceptions to the rules. Maybe you are a wife who doesn't talk much; maybe your husband enjoys chatting. The point is, the two of you use different means to feel connected and thus show connection to each other in different ways. Knowing how your spouse prefers to connect can help you engage better on more meaningful levels. It's not one way or another. You have to be willing to explore the other person's way so that rediscovery and reconnection can be made. In order to love well, sometimes we have to disconnect ourselves from our preferences, so that we can do things in a manner that means the most to our spouse. This requires conversation over assumptions. You have to be willing to ask the questions and explore each other's needs regarding what each of you need in order to feel loved and connected, what can be done to show care and what can be done to be more intentional in the relationship moving forward. These conversations should be had on a regular basis to reconnect and rediscover each other's feelings, wants and needs. Unless we ask the questions, we'll never know the answers. That was my problem in my newlywed months. Because Jarrett wasn't engaging with me the way I thought he was supposed to, I thought he wasn't interested. I was looking for him to respond in the same ways that I did, not taking into account that he was expressing his love in ways that he felt most comfortable doing. After a while, I started to feel lonely and began to explore other means of connection with other things that I could control like personal projects, talking on the phone, shopping and social media. I figured, if he's not going to engage with me, then I'll find something else to engage with. So, while he'd check the sports stats, I'd check in with my cousins and friends. He'd pull me close and stroke my hair, but he wouldn't say much – not to my liking, so I very wrongly assumed that this was a confirmation in his disinterest in connection. Ironically, he thought we were bonding well! He thought our time spent together was proof that we were connecting. He was happy to share time and space together in silence, while I was longing for conversations that explored deep thoughts. Neither one of us had a clue about the other's feelings because we were living in assumptions and our feelings regulated themselves based on those perceptions.

One day, we were cuddled on the couch on a lazy afternoon. He had pulled me close as he was watching ESPN. Neither one of us were speaking and the feeling of loneliness overwhelmed me. I didn't know what he was thinking, and I wasn't sure how to express how I was feeling. A few tears fell from my eyes and onto his arm and He immediately turned off the TV, sat me up and asked me what was the matter? This was one of the most sincere and special conversations we had during our first months of marriage. It was through this talk that we both realized we needed to connect to each other in different ways than what we were naturally akin to. Jarrett felt very connected with me just because of proximity and I, on the other hand, felt something was wrong because we weren't talking. We both realized that in order to truly connect to one another, we needed to be more intentional about disconnecting from our own way of comfort in order to reconnect to each other in manners that meant most.

Since then, I now understand that being physically close to Jarrett fills his heart and he has been more intentional about starting conversations with me by not just listening, but also contributing. He will often ask me how I'm feeling and if there is anything I need from him, which I think is so attentive! He doesn't always notice when I need a good dive into verbal romance and I sometimes forget that he is an introvert and better expresses himself with gestures than with words, but we are learning. It's only been seven years, after all! We've still many miles to go before we're through; but talking about our needs has certainly helped us realize that we both need different things, and that's ok. Sometimes, we have to lay our preferences to the side in order to reconnect to our spouse. Disconnect to reconnect. What a fabulous idea!

Blessings Not Blaming

I don't know about you, but 2020 has created some crazy opportunities to have all sorts of discussions. Like you, my family and I are stuck at home right now. COVID-19 has us cooped up in the house and I am growing weary. It's not that I am ready to get back to life as "normal", whatever that means, but honestly, I started running out of ideas for my children. The first three months or so, we had a nice routine: breakfast, morning work for Kailyn, ABC's and color recognition for Jaelle, story time, French lessons, snack and Sesame Street, nap time, lunch after nap, crafts after lunch, family walk, outdoor play time, PBS Kids while I cooked dinner, eat dinner, movie and dessert, Bible Story, family prayer, night-night.

That's what we did, day after day, and I was feeling rather accomplished about it … that is until all the craft paper ran out and the glue dried up and Jaelle decided she'd rather eat the Crayola's for lunch instead of her sandwich. I'm sure I cried every single day in the month of May! June finally came around and it rained for two weeks in a row, and with nowhere to go, I felt incapable and overwhelmed. Jarrett had conference calls most of the day, the girls were so bored, and I was exhausted. Amazon was backed up; Target was lacking in supplies and I was over it! On one particular day, the rain was so awful, and the girls were so loud, I went to desperate measures: a Disney Movie Marathon! We watched many of the classics all afternoon and into dinner time. I admit, that was probably a major "Bad-Mom" moment: watching hours of screen, stuffing our faces with cookies and hot chocolate, in our PJs, but I am human, and I needed some sanity.

We ended our couch coasting session with Beauty and the Beast, at Jarrett's request! It's my husband's favorite Disney film and such a sweet story! I love it, too, and seeing it for the first time with our girls was absolutely wonderful! All cuddled up together on the couch, I began to take notice of the scene where the Beast rescues Belle from the wolves. He was wounded from his efforts and she was trying to bandage him up by the fireplace. They were both cold and wet and in their own degree of pain. Both were trying to help the other in their own way. Both were frustrated and both began with such good intensions, but somehow, an argument managed to break out between them. It's that old familiar struggle we all fall into at some time in our marriage: misunderstandings.

"That hurts!", the Beast hollers.

"Well, if you would hold still it wouldn't hurt as much!", Belle persists.

"Well, if you hadn't run away, this wouldn't have happened."

"You shouldn't have yelled at me."

"You shouldn't have gone into the West Wing."

"You should learn to control your temper."

That's usually how it goes, doesn't it? Two well intentioned people, unable to get their genuine intents across to the other. How many times have we been in that exact situation in our marriage? How many times have we tried to institute healing only to be misunderstood? How many times have our husbands tried to make things right with us, only for us to point out what they did wrong?Sweet friends, the blame game gets us nowhere. Valuable bonding opportunities are burned to the ground when we choose to blame one another. It's one of those lessons often learned in hindsight, but if we can consider what's at stake and how our communication can help alleviate the tension, I think we will better notice the blessings in it all: that we are married to men who love us, that we've been entrusted to nurture and love our families alongside our husbands and that our love can be a shining example to inspire others and proclaim the goodness of God.

I think at the core of us all, we desire to be fully known and fully loved. But the depths of us belongs only to God. See, when I look at Jarrett, I know that he loves me fully, but knowing me fully … not so much. Of course, he knows the essence of who I am. He knows my personality, my interests, my fears and my hopes. He knows my favorite ice cream, my best friends, my quirks and my red flags, but he cannot know what I am unable to reveal to him. If I am to be honest, there are parts of myself that confuse even me and there are corners of my heart that I can barely grasp or understanding, myself. The Bible tells us that no one knows their own heart entirely (Jeremiah 17:9). Since this is true, it's unfair that I expect Jarrett to understand me fully when I don't even know myself completely. This is why communication is so vital. I cannot just expect my husband to "get me", understand me or interpret my intentions or feelings without help. If I don't understand all of me, I cannot expect him to. I have to be humble enough and sometimes even courageous enough to allow the Lord to search my heart (Psalm 139:23) and then have the faith required to expose my heart to my husband and share my feelings and thoughts in efforts to inform him on areas that neither of us may have been aware of. When this doesn't happen, it's so easy to get frustrated and feel misunderstood. Though I know I am fully loved by my husband, the lack of being fully known can be hurtful, and let's be honest, when we are hurting, we start blaming.

Getting to the place where we no longer expect our husbands to read our minds and know our intentions will free us to communicate in more loving ways. The statement, "If you loved me then you would understand me", is so false ladies, and I think we know it. I think we know full well that our men can never understand us completely, because they are men! They weren't created to see and sense and seek out the world the way we do. They aren't supposed to. Their masculinity gives them a different viewpoint on life and love and though they cherish us, they did not create us. God is the only One who understands us fully, because He made us, and He alone truly knows us (Psalm 139:1). He knows the depths of us, beyond even our own understanding, yet He has given us grace to intently seek and discover one another. It's called honest communication, and it can help us align our hearts and minds with our spouses by focusing on what's true. Honest communication allows us to see beyond the moment and truly count our blessings and when we are more aware of our blessings we blame less, and we are better equipped to bless more.

The more we share our hearts, the more we posture ourselves to bless instead of blame. When we count our blessings, we are able to speak them out. But I do get it. I've been married long enough to be guilty of impulsively blaming. I have certainly pointed my finger at Jarrett for areas I perceived to be his fault. I have accused him of not caring about me or not understanding me. But that doesn't solve problems, it creates tension and offense. This is the exact opposite of what any of us desire. So how can we reroute our communication styles to ensure that our discussions create environments of resolution, respect and harmony? We start by blessing instead of blaming. Instead of waiting for our husbands to figure it out, we, being mature women in the Lord, can begin uncovering ourselves in invitation to their exploration of how we are feeling and thinking and intending. Instead of pointing fingers at them for misunderstanding us, we can open our arms for an embrace and encourage open and healthy communication, even if that means we have to take the lead. Instead of recalculating missteps, we can express our appreciation for our husbands' efforts and invite him to share his feelings with confidence. This is how we invite them into our inner hearts. This is how we avoid unnecessary arguments and tension. No one is a mind reader. If you cannot predict his every move, there's no way he can predict yours, either. Honesty helps us eliminates the urge to blame each other for unnecessary things. Give blessings instead. Affirm his efforts and praise his intentions because sincere blessings have ways of bridging over the tension that misunderstandings aim to create.

<u>Inspiration for Communication</u>

The "togetherness" of marriage does not automatically create closeness. Breathing under the same roof doesn't guarantee connectivity or confidence. You have to develop that by making time to connect in deeper ways. All this means is that if you want to know what he's thinking about and what's going on in his mind, you need to carve out time in your day to seek out those inner experiences— exciting moments that happened at work, funny things the kids said, the latest news with family or friends. These conversations inspire us to seek out the moments of our day that meant the most to each of us. It might not look like holding hands and looking deeply into one another's eyes, under moonlight with dripping candles dancing all around us, but that's ok. Connecting has little to do with the ambiance and more to do with calculated intentionality. Maybe he's more approachable when the workday is done. Maybe he's more engaging after the kids have gone to bed. Remember, in order to discover, you have to meet a person where they are, and it takes trial and error. You won't always get perfect responses, and that's ok. Love is not about perfect pictures, it's about authentic moments.

Being flexible is so important, because every day holds different experiences and the varieties of our experiences often effect our mood. Sometimes, the morning is a better time to talk than in the evening. Sometimes, a phone call is more manageable than a late-night couch session. No matter the means of communication, the important thing is that we stay willing and inspired to connect in the opportunities that we intentionally carve out for our spouse. In time, you will find what works best for your relationship and these conversations will forge an intimate knowledge of each other, which is the ultimate goal.

"Then I shall know fully, even as I have been fully known."
-1 Corinthians 13:12 (ESV)

This is what we all want in our marriages: To be known. We may not always be understood, but we can inspire one another to dig deeper into the heart of who we are and into the essence of our experiences because healthy and meaningful communication keeps a relationship current and intentional. Some men, including mine, may have some struggles to open up and go "deep", but give them patience and ask questions that require a detailed answer, not just a "yes" or "no" response. In turn, don't have contempt for learning a new activity that your husband enjoys in order to create comfortable atmosphere that are suitable for conversation. Don't feel anxious if his way of connection needs to begin with shoulder to shoulder time. He isn't avoiding you; it's his way of pulling you close.

On days where I've joined Jarrett on the golf course, he asks me to drive the cart and make stops at each hole. He'll hit the ball and just looks up into space, trying to estimate where it might land. Each time the ball drops, he looks at me with this huge smile and I do a little golf clap for him. These are such fun afternoons for us both and his happiness nudges his chattiness! I've learned that activities motivate his conversation. It's not very natural for him to sit on the couch and share unbridled thoughts with me, but if he's out and about, doing something invigorating, those are environments where he's more apt to open up. Over the years, he has greatly improved at mulling over his thoughts with me in the middle of a quiet night. He's learning to pull me close and listen to me expound on my never-ending thoughts and he's also learning to chime in with his own perspective and viewpoint. I cannot begin to express how happy these moments make me! We've each needed to learn one another's communication styles so that we can get the most of our time and out of opportunities to connect. It took some time to get to this place in our marriage, but I am so grateful for the growth in our communication and understanding.

It's not always seamless, but the effort can be monumental! If need be, learn to enjoy the silence of his company or muster up your courage to take on activities that you may not naturally be interested in. Initiate adventures that will fuel later conversations. There are great discoveries waiting for you both and your willingness can inspire more meaningful moments to come. You don't have to settle for mundane familiarity; take the plunge to explore the depths of your husband and encourage him to do the same with you. It might look different from day to day, month to month, year to year and that's ok. Sometimes, it will consist of you focusing on his needs and sometimes it will consist of him focusing on your needs, but either way, it's mutually beneficial to the health and wellness of your marriage and will inspire you both to love deeper and know each other more fully.

<u>Speaking Life</u>

Naturally, it wasn't until Belle thanked the Beast for his kindness in saving her life that the argument dwindled. Isn't that interesting? They would have kept going back and forth and probably passed out from exhaustion, but someone had to choose to break the blames by offering up a blessing.

"Thank you", she said. That's all it took to soften moods and soften hearts. "I'm sorry", is also very powerful, too. It's a sign of humility and self-lessness, which yields an environment that's ripe for peace and harmony. Pride prevents productivity. If we want to grow, if we want abundance, then we've got to say the loving things. We cannot hold onto our self-righteousness or our pride if we desire to cultivate marriages that produce emotionally harmonious havens.

The Bible tells us that a soft answer turns away wrath (Proverbs 15:1) and that we should be quick to listen, slow to speak and slow to become angry (Proverbs 18:21) because human anger (frustration, annoyances, irritation) does not bring about righteousness (James 1:20). These scriptures imply that there are times when arguments will occur, and sometimes heated ones at that, still we must love. Did you know that you are spiritually responsible for every word that you speak (Matthew 12: 36)? Our words make impacts. They can lull away tension or they can ignite it. Note in the second scripture, Proverbs 18:21, where The Lord instructs us to be slow to speak. This isn't suggesting that we change frequency in the volume of our speech, but rather that we consider carefully what we are going to say by analysing our words before we speak them to ensure that there is no fault in them. How many tears could be saved if we all paused before we spoke, listened before we reacted and craved the longevity of harmony rather than the momentary satisfaction of self-expression?

When we don't listen, speak too fast and are easily offended, we are sure to say something destructive. This is unwise ladies, and it is very selfish and foolish. Wisdom always looks into the future (Proverbs 24:14). She understands that her choices today will carve out her tomorrow. She doesn't fling her words around carelessly (Proverbs 17:27) or react too hastily without first seeking understanding (Proverbs 3:13), because, according to the Bible, wisdom cultivates peace (Proverbs 3:17). A woman who desires to love well desires the wisdom to speak well. It is so important that we have empathy and kindness as we communicate and have dialogue with our husbands, because blaming gets us nowhere. It runs us around in futile circles with nothing to show for ourselves besides hot air and useless results. We've been called to live higher than that and so we must speak words that reflect the magnitude of who we are in Christ. Applying such wisdom will save us from the chaos of suppositions and assumptions which can lead us into unnecessary arguments. Scripture gives us a better tactic. It teaches us that death and life are in the power of the tongue (Proverbs 18:21). This obviously suggests that we have a choice in which we choose to speak: life or death?

Speaking life is wisdom and it's a game changer. It's not only for the benefit of your husband to build him up emotionally and spiritually, but to also remind you of all the wonderful gifts God has blessed you with through your union with your man. We must be willing to nurture and convey our words in order to uplift our husbands concerning their personal and spiritual growth and their efforts to be good men, good husbands, fathers and friends. It's these daily exchanges of love that fuels our marriages in impactful ways. We have a choice to speak life or death. I want us to choose life.

There is no excuse when it comes to the words we choose to say and every single sentence we speak or have ever spoken will be judged by Jesus Christ (Matthew 12:36). Heavy, I know, but I want you to consider your conversations in light of eternity. Your marriage is sacred, therefore using wisdom to formulate your words is so imperative because wisdom always chooses the loving thing. Words spoken without love can destroy my day and ultimately destroy me in the process. There is nothing more disparaging than the aftermaths of a bad argument when unloving words have been spoken and opportunities for harmony and forgiveness weren't taken into account. The lingering results tear at the seams of any relationship, including within our marriages, which breaks down trust and a sense of safety. It makes you feel so low and icky and completely deflated. It does the same to the other person and it causes divides, which do not come from God.

"The wise woman builds her house, but with her own hands the foolish one tears hers down" -Proverbs 14:1 (ESV)

Think about your words like you would think about bricks on your home. Speaking negatively, blaming, cursing and belittling words are like removing a brick from your own home. In time, the whole thing will surely come crumbling down and odds are, you might get hit with a few bricks in the process. We must decide to choose our words carefully and carefully examine our intentions behind the words we are speaking. This doesn't mean we should be coddling or sugar coating our conversations. What it does mean is that we should be speaking with the intent to better our relationship rather than merely making our point. Whenever we share the truth in love by speaking life, it results in lifting others up and showing appreciation, even when we disagree. We can say what we think and speak hard truths in a manner that doesn't depreciate others. We can speak lifegiving words that are truthful and loving at the same time (Ephesians 4:15). This will not only encourage our husbands but will also protect our marriages.

Discussing Your Discussions

Like you, I have a core group of friends that I confide in. We're all married and have known each other for many years. It's so refreshing to have girlfriends that you can share and experience the various stages of life with and glean advice from. But in my seven years of marriage, I have had to make the choice to be selective about what I share concerning my husband. I do confide in my friends about family issues and struggles I am having as a mother and a wife, but negative thoughts or concerns that I have about Jarrett as a person – I guard those thoughts because I do not want a slip of my tongue to give anyone the false perception to think lowly of my husband. He is my gift, so I protect my husband's honor at all costs. This doesn't mean that I conceal my struggles or deny them, but I have learned that there is a distinct difference between talking about a person and talking about a problem. Problems are great discussions to have because we all need support and advice; but talking about a person is a whole different matter, particularly when the person is your husband.

It's so natural to run to our friends with updates on our highs and lows. A listening ear is often the comfort we need to dump all our issues and concerns out. True friendships consist of vulnerable moments, but when those moments take a turn into negative chatter, we have to be careful. Sadly, I've been in the presence of women who've felt the need to speak discouragingly about their husbands over issues they can't seem to resolve. It can easily be brushed off as a venting session, but discussing negative opinions concerning your husband needs to be addressed with him and not with others. Everything doesn't need to be known by everyone and it's important that we take care of our marriages by guarding certain matters. When we find ourselves speaking in negative and belittling ways about our men, this can be so damaging because bashing, blaming, belittling and disrespectful name calling is the exact opposite of speaking life and it should have no place in our conversations.

"Let no unwholesome word proceed from your mouth, but only such a word as is good for edification according to the need of the moment, so that it will give grace to those who hear." -Ephesians 4:29 (NIV)

Even if your opinion of your husband is at an all-time low, you can still be loving enough to protect and respect the privacy of his trust in you and in your marriage. Your best friend cares, but her relationship with you is not sacred. Using wisdom on what to share and what to protect is of upmost importance as we make steps to reinstate harmony in place of frustrations or disagreements. Sometimes, the healthy thing to do is to not discuss your discussions with outside people. Instead, when the time is right, revisit the topic together at a later time. In this way, you won't have outside opinions buzzing in your ear to further complicate matters that should be handled within the privacy of your marriage.

As we all soon find out, marriage is a complicated existence. I want to encourage us all to be determined in thinking on things that are lovely and true (Philippians 4:8) and share information with your friends and family only with intentions of getting sound advice rather than for outlets of criticism. Use your discussions to remind yourself of how valuable your marriage is and seek audience with people who you know will affirm your marriage and encourage you in loving well. There are just too many people, in the name of friendship, who will take your concerns as their opportunity to bash your man. How many times have we heard the comment, "Girl, you don't need him.", "Girl, how do you put up with that?", "Girl, you deserve better." Such advice does not come from love or truth. You may never have experienced a conversation like this, personally, but we've been around discussions where someone has directed similar statements towards someone else's husband. There are just some women who have no problem putting men down because our culture encourages it. Don't give anyone permission to speak these lies into your life or into your marriage.

Listen, anyone who undermines your husband's value is not your friend. Anyone who cheers you on to disrespect your husband or advocates you to disregard your marriage does not have godly love in mind. Your marriage is sacred, no matter what your husband has done or what the two of you are going through. As long as you are married, you are in covenant and this is such a precious existence between a man and a woman. Never let anyone trample on this, not even in the name of friendship. Allowing or engaging in such negative affirmations is unwise and unhealthy and those of us who have the gift of gab need to use wisdom when it comes to what we share and who we share it with. A true friend will always advise you in prayer. A true friend will encourage you and point you in the direction of resolving conflicts, restoring harmony and forgiving always. A true friend gives good guidance that encourages you to love your husband well and will remind you of your husband's love for you. Any comment that creates thoughts outside of those parameters is evil advice.

I am passionate about encouraging you in your lows and in your highs because God is always at work (John 13:7). There is no situation that He cannot save. There is no marriage that could ever forfeit His blessings. Sweet friends, I am cheering you on to trust Jesus with every conversation, thought, words, tears, fears, joys ... because the love of Christ is at work. Don't give anyone permission to tear down what the Lord is building in your life. This is why I am also a firm believer that married women should make the choice to seek council from other married women. Your single friend cannot advise you well in your marriage. She's never taken vows; she's never been in covenant. Wisdom seeks out wisdom and there are too many women who are taking bad advice from inexperienced people. Single women, I urge you to make the same decision. If you desire to prepare yourself for marriage, I am charging you to seek your relationship advice from a married woman who has a proven record of loving well. Don't ask Google. Don't ask The Real Housewives. Don't ask Marie Claire. Don't ask your single friends about marital matters. How can someone advise you in areas they themselves have no experience in? Seek instruction from women who you know have grown spiritually and who mirror the marriage that you desire to cultivate for yourself.

"Fools give full vent to their rage, but the wise bring calm in the end."
-Proverbs 29:11 (NLT)

Good advice produces calmness and clarity, not chaos. Take heed of that, because when you choose to receive wise marital advice, it will encourage you to draw closer to your husband so the two of you can continue to produce deeper and flourishing love in peaceful and godly ways. These lessons go further than mere flattery. Wisdom is genuine and requires your keen observation concerning what is and what is not appropriate to share and receive.

The Bible urges us to guard our tongues (Proverbs 13:13), to guard our minds (Colossians 3:2) and our hearts (Proverbs 4:23). Remember, your marriage is always going to be a work in progress. Every discussion you have should help strengthen your marriage and place you in better position to love well and deeply. A venting session out of momentary frustration isn't worth it. Rather than using our words to put down our husbands, we can remind ourselves of our husband's efforts in the marriage. What is your husband doing that is praiseworthy? What is it about your husband that you are truly thankful for? Gossip takes no thought, but keenly examining the efforts and the growth of your husband can produce soul stirring conversations (1 Corinthians 13:5).

As you take note of praiseworthy efforts, speak these things and use them as a base for your outside discussions. Focus on his efforts over his failures and invest in friendships that will advocate for your union. We can all do a better job of looking past the faults in order to recognize growth and effort. It's all in our perspective. He may have left the milk out all night, but he did feed the baby because he wanted you to get some extra sleep; be sure to thank him for his thoughtfulness instead of blaming him for his forgetfulness. Maybe he spent too much time in the yard, but he's digging up earth so that your home can be as beautiful and welcoming on the outside as you have made it on the inside. Maybe he didn't make the reservations in enough time, but he did make time for you and wants to spend his life with you. And maybe He's not joining every Bible study like you are, but he is taking notes in church and he is growing in his faith. A shift in perspective can make all the difference; the discussions you are having about your husband will affect the perspective you practice.

The positive things he is doing needs your blessing and these are the discussions we should be having in between the conflicts and the disagreements. As his wife, you have the unique opportunity to speak words over him that no other woman has the privilege of doing; not his mother, not his sister, not his grandma or his auntie; you and only you. Don't waste that gift! Celebrate his efforts and the next time you're out with friends, brag on your man a little! Find something you're grateful for and share it. Slip in a good story about him to highlight his strengths and then go home and tell him all about the complements you shared. When you are around his friends and family, bless your husband in their midst. Complement the man he is and the man he is becoming. These are the better discussions to have. These are the words that we should be sharing.

<u>Creating Deeper Trust</u>

As we progress in our communication and discoveries within our marriages, we may begin to also uncover new truths within ourselves. Remember, we are always changing and becoming. We grow from girlfriends, to wives, to mothers and each season brings its fair share of change. This is also true for our husbands. It's so important to take notice of our own growth so that we can then communicate these discoveries with each other. It can be unnerving, but it takes courage and intentionality to enhance trust in so that we can share our ever-changing selves without fear or intimidation. Honest communication makes this possible and it's not always easy or comfortable. Sometimes, there are hard things that need to be said – honest, raw, vulnerable and intimate truths that we must address, first in ourselves and then in each other. It's so very easy to put these things off, but I must advise us all that doing so won't spare you an argument, it could cost you trust.

Please keep in mind that trust occurs through the unveiling of truth. There will never be trust where there is no truth. A woman who desires to love well is willing to do the difficult thing, risk her comfort zone, risk her reputation, risk her picture-perfect allure, and even risk her tears, all for the sake of sharing the truth in love. If we are unwilling to unveil who we are, we cannot expect to truly be loved for all that we are. I know this can be so scary. Considering that we live in a world that teaches us to bury the pain, cover up what's ugly and deny what's true. It can feel daunting for some us to consider sharing deep thoughts and feelings, even with our husbands, but trust requires it. Trust demands it.

We cannot cover up truth in our marriages and expect to cultivate trust; not if we want to love deeply and live freely. Remember, the truth will set you free (John 8:32)! Covering up, avoiding, hiding, excusing … these things are not loving. They are self-preservation mechanisms that are used in order to not have to face ourselves; let alone allow others to do the same. Humility, however, beacons us to expose the hidden things in order to build greater trust because great marriages are built on the consistency of growing trust. Trust can't be altered, manipulated or faked. Real trust is genuine and unquestionable. The trust you had in year one will not sustain you in year ten. You have to nourish trust in your marriage so that it can produce growth and sustain the change. Without an intrinsic trust in marriage, the both of you will suffocate.

So, how do we use our conversations to develop trust in our marriages? I believe that trust is developed through two intentional manners: observation and invitation. We can develop trust when we both observe each other making trustworthy decisions and when we invite one another into our intimate space. When we are consistent in our promises, sexually faithful, and supportive of our home, our marriage thrives. None of these feats are wow-factors. It's basic and expected, but it does produce positive results and builds observable trust which often times is less threatening to express.

Observable trust doesn't require us to go above or beyond. It's predictable behavior, day in and day out. For example, I know that if I choose to stay within our budget and not use our light bill money for my personal spending, Jarrett will notice my financial discipline and will see me as trustworthy with our income. I've not done anything wonderful, yet my observable actions will result in a wonderful response in his confidence and faith in me. Another example could be sexual. We all know that monogamy is imperative for trust in a relationship. If we are sexually faithful to our husbands – not flirting with other men, not going off to explore other relationships within our marriage – this will also build trust. Again, we've not done anything extraordinary. Quite frankly, we've done the minimal of what is respectful and what's expected by staying true to our husband, but this behavior is observable, and it benefits the marriage and produces trust. Though observable trust is very important, think of it like a boxed cake: it's easy, it's convenient and it isn't very challenging. Observable trust certainly has a place and value, but if this is the only canopy in which we are developing trust, we limit our love from the depths of discovery and becoming.

Over time, as we grow and change in life, our priorities and needs will also change, however, they may not be as easily visible, therefore could become more complicated to observe. Changes such as these can sometimes have serious impacts on the relationship. Sharing these new truths is so very imperative so that the two of you will stay in unity and make necessary decisions concerning issues and interests that may evolve as you grow. For example, if there has been disappointment for any matter of reasons and it's not been resolved, it must be spoken and addressed. Such hurt needs healing and healing will never result from depressing the truth or avoiding a conversation. We cannot take the frame of mind that it will just go away or that our spouse should realize our internal disappointments. In cases such as these, we can build trust through inviting our spouse to explore the areas that observable measures won't reveal. It's fine if things don't easily bother you or cause you concern, but when they do, we have to be mature enough to take the initiative through invitation so that matters of concern can be revealed and addressed in timely and appropriate ways.

Building invitational trust could involve sharing personal changes that may have developed over time. For instance, let's say both of you married with the intentions of having multiple children but one person later realizes they now only want one child. This needs to be discussed. Or, what about spiritual growth? Perhaps the church you've been attending is no longer providing what one of you may need for your growth and maturity. It's so easy to say nothing and hope things get better, but inviting your spouse into your concerns and feelings will help build trust as the two of you seek God for new directions and new seasons that the Lord may be leading the two of you in (Psalm 32:8).

There are so many other scenarios we could consider, but the point is that changes such as these are internal and less likely to be observable. They can be very scary to talk about and could result in rocking the boat of comfort, but a comfortable boat won't sail very far. No one wants to shift routine. No one enjoys messing up what's comfortable, but sometimes it's very necessary and can prove to be quite beneficial in the relevancy of your relationship. Your instinct may be to keep it a secret until you figure it out, but that's not team playing. That's not trusting your husband, that's trusting yourself to take care of an issue that the two of you should be solving, together. Inevitably, this could have reverse affects and weaken the trust that you are truly desiring to build. There is nothing worse than finding out that your spouse kept something from you. It can make that person feel inferior, left out and devalued – all characteristics that kill trust.

This is why developing trust through invitation is just as essential and displaying observational trust. I'll warn you, though, cultivating invitational trust can feel more risky than observational trust because it requires us to unveil ourselves in vulnerable and exposed ways. Building trust by invitation is often times uncomfortable, risky, and takes intentionality by opening up about what's happening in our inner lives: our thoughts, feelings, hopes, dreams, fears, struggles, disappointments and even our anger. These changes don't always surface naturally. We have to choose to expose them, and I believe that being open and honest about these things creates a proactive approach to building wonderful trust in our marriages. Deeper trust leads to more confidence and confidence creates security in our love; without this, it's quite difficult for any relationship to flourish beyond a surfaced cordiality.

Building trust in your marriage is a joy you can learn to cultivate. So many of us are walking around with anxieties, concerns, hidden hopes and uncertainties. We need to let our men in on what is happening inside of us. Remember that he is your husband. There is no other person on this earth that will love you more. We must actually trust them if we desire to grow with them and inviting them into our inner space will strengthen our marriages. I know, as wives, we sometimes worry about not being understood by our husbands or stressing them out in some way. That's a common fear and though this sentiment is noteworthy, not telling your husband what you need or how you feel will keep the relationship from growing and advancing.

Fusing All the Pieces

Once you can celebrate that you are a woman in progress and that changes are constantly stirring within you, you will be better equipped to dive deeper into discovery within your marriage, for your husband and for yourself. I urge us all to find the courage to let our husbands in on what we are dealing with in our inner most hearts. He needs to hear about it. Trusting him and procuring deeper trust in your marriage requires honesty. Keeping quiet out of fear never anyone, and I challenge that our fears arise because we struggle with trust.

The best way to drive out fear and grow your trust in one another is to just be honest. In some cases, healthy communication might require seeking outside help, as in a counselor, a pastor or a therapist. Take this advice or leave it, but if you woke up one morning with difficulty breathing, you would call the doctor, wouldn't you? Trust and communication are the oxygen for marriage. No matter how healthy the heart is, without oxygen, the quality of life will be compromised. If you'll seek professional help for a physical concern, it's only logical to seek professional help for a marital concern that you have been unable to resolve yourself. This doesn't have to be negative; this could be very positive and healthy. It's all in your perspective and in your desire to grow and build trust together. Sometimes, it truly does take an outside source to help you fuse the puzzle pieces together. I know many loving and happy couples that have gone this route.

During our first year of marriage, Jarrett and I continued our pre-marital sessions into post-marriage sessions with my Father. We used this safe space to address new terrains that all newlyweds encounter, and we gained wonderful, monthly advice. I have no doubts that we jumped over many hurtles simply by placing ourselves under godly mentorship. The questions posed to us (that we didn't realize needed to be asked) helped us to better understand our family histories and personalities as well as one another's perspectives on life in a more clarified way. It's up to you and your husband on how or when or if you seek help, but don't write it off. There's a reason why God created counselors and it's something to consider if you desire more openness in ways you may be struggling tap into on your own. If counseling isn't something you're comfortable with, you should take inventory of influential couples in your life. Do you have mentors —friends or family who you are reaching out to for godly wisdom and advice? If not, why? You can't do this alone. If there is a marriage that you admire, reach out and begin to glean from them. Ask them about their marriage and take time to invest in learning from them. Their wisdom can help you navigate your marriage and equip you for maturity in your pursuits of loving well.

Though we are all different, taking the necessary measures to develop truthful conversation is one thing that we all should be working towards. If neither spouse is willing to dive into unveiling discussions, someone is going to get lost. If no one is talking, then no one is listening and that is an ugly train wreck just waiting to happen. Sometimes, it does take a professional perspective to help us procure the vital questions that need to be discussed. This is up to you, but conversations about what we are experiencing isn't optional– not if you desire to love well and grow deeper. I get that not everyone is comfortable with talking to someone they don't know, but there are so many resources such as books, conferences, and classes at church that could help you identify how to say what needs to be said. It's judgmental to hold each other responsible for not meeting needs and expectations that aren't being discussed. Talking can be scary, but loving well pushes past the discomfort to exercise trust. Wise women not only know this, they understand it and they implement it (James 1: 22-23). So, I encourage you to take the time to continue to develop honest communication with your husband. Don't worry about scaring him off. You have his ring and he has your heart. God is taking you both into new depths and territory with every fresh discovery He is unearthing in you both. Give each other a front row seat to all your self-discoveries, changes and trust. It always starts with a conversation and will spark new interest and permeate new anticipation in your marriage for years to come.

Reflection

Throughout your day, how are you using your words to connect and uplift your husband and your marriage?

<u>Scriptures for Your Soul</u>

"A gentle tongue is a tree of life, but perverseness in it breaks the spirit."
- Proverbs 15:4

"The good person out of the good treasure of his heart produces good, and the evil person out of his evil treasure produces evil, for out of the abundance of the heart the mouth speaks."
-Luke 6:4

CHAPTER 5

THE OTHER SIDE OF LOVING

A few years ago, I decided to try a new hairstylist. I wanted to get my hair straightened and so I did some searching online and took a chance on a salon in our art district. The stylist was very talented and detailed, but I felt so awkward sitting in that chair with wet hair, listening to a stranger berating her poor husband and calling him names. I just sat there silently bewildered, as she sudsed and cut and pulled on my hair. What's worse, the other girls in the salon were co-signing her contempt and disrespect, making jokes and matters worse. It was such an uncomfortable experience.

I'm sure this advice is not a new concept for any of us, but publicly shaming your man is not going to benefit your marriage or help it grow and bloom in deeper ways. What it will do is permeate negativity in your thought patterns and give permission for others to affirm those negative thoughts. We've hinted on this a bit earlier, but we're going to take some deeper looks into honoring our marriages, according to God's Word. Having clarity concerning respect is vital, so I want to be the kind of friend that gives you honesty as well as encouragement when it comes to loving well.

"Each man must love his wife as he loves himself,
and the wife must respect her husband."
-Ephesians 5: 33 (NLT)

The word "must" is an instruction, not a suggestion, and although the charge to love seems more important than the instruction to respect, I want to emphasize that respect is fuel for love. A beautiful Lamborghini is only lawn décor if there is no fuel in the gas chamber. Your marriage isn't going anywhere without genuine respect. It's not going to grow; it's not going to advance or shine or impact without the fuel of respect. It not only fuels love in a marriage, it also propagates a response of godly submission towards our husbands, as scripture also instructs every wife to do (Ephesians 5: 22). Therefore, the combination of respect and submission formulates honor – a virtue that not only signifies trust but also initiates intimacy.

Respect and submission can be daunting words that many of us struggle with; particularly "submission". It's that scary anti-feminist term we're told is medieval and chauvinistic. Don't be afraid of the word submission, friends. If it's in the Good Book, then it's good for you and our Heavenly Father will never give us, let alone ask us to do something for our harm or detriment (James 1:7). Because He designed marriage, God knows what will embolden a successful one. Remember, marriage isn't about us finding a good man to make us feel good – that's performance, which is selfish and shallow. Being a loving wife of noble character entails us pouring out into our husbands just as much and as frequently as we desire them to pour into us. Respecting our husbands while in submission to their godly leadership is the ultimate way of pouring into a man and doing so is a blessing for our marriages and obedience to God. It's something that our husbands need from us, therefore it's something that our marriages need, as well.

Whether a husband deserves respect or not, a flourishing marriage does not practice disrespect. I don't care what your co-worker is telling you, disrespect for any reasons is wrong. Whether it be the silent treatment, rebelliously doing something you know would offend him or simply cutting him down in your mind over a forced dinner, disrespect isn't loving, and it will not propel your marriage. A woman who desires to love well understands that love does not dishonour others (1 Corinthians 13: 5-7), it does not belittle (Proverbs 12:18), nor does it puff itself up with pride (Romans 11:21). Rather, God's love is patient and kind. It is not proud or rude or easily angered. It doesn't enjoy evil, but celebrates what is true. It always uplifts, protects and hopes. It's selfless, other-focused, respectful and submissive to God's love (1 Corinthians 13: 1-7). Is this how you're intentionally loving your husband? Does your love look like 1st Corinthians, chapter 13? Be encouraged that none of us love perfectly, but the perfect love of Jesus can be applied to our lives and therefore implemented in our marriages to produce such intentionality in our loving. It starts with Salvation because Jesus can isn't limited to just saving our souls; He can save our love, as well!

<u>How Do We Do This?</u>

As women who desire to love well, we know it takes God's love to love in godly ways. God's love transforms our hearts as well as our lives and it's this transformation that affects our application because the love of Jesus changes everything. His love will not only change our understanding of love but also our demonstration of love for Him, for our husband and for others in our lives. It's His love that makes the mission of marriage possible and part of that mission is to respect and submit to our husbands.

"Wives, submit to your husbands as to the Lord. For the husband is the head of the wife as Christ is the head of the church, his body, of which he is the Savior. As the church submits to Christ, so wives should submit to their husbands in everything." -Ephesians 5:22-24 (NIV)

Whether you are aware of it or not, we all submit to something every day. No one is independently living their lives without the influence of something or someone. Spiritually speaking, scripture tells us that we are either in submission to God or to sin (Matthew 6:24). We're either intentionally making choices that honor the Lord or we are intentionally making choices that honor this world. In its simplicity, submission basically means to honor the influence of another person by aligning yourself in agreement with them. This is obedience in its purest form. It's something that God requires and something He's placed in a man to desire.

The truth is that you and your husband should be an influence over each other in your marriage. We certainly want to influence our men to express their love to us in various ways such as emotionally, with their time, compliments and maybe even gifts. But understand that your husband desires your love to be expressed towards him as respect. Submission makes respect authentic. Of course, there are always exceptions to the innate needs of men and women, but according to a study completed by Emerson Eggerichs, PhD., 74% of men identified respect as a reflection of love.[10] This doesn't mean that women do not desire or need respect as well, but in many cases, for a man, the preference of love displayed through respect overrides the preference of displaying love emotionally the way many women prefer. Therefore, a refusal of submission within marriage is a withholding of both love and respect in the perspective of many men. At times, disrespect may even translate as, "I'm choosing not to show you love."

Listen, I know this goes against practically everything society tells us about our rights as women and about love and sex and confidence, but how society handles its affairs will never be in line with God's standards or His blessings for you (Isaiah 55: 8-9). There is a reason for every instruction God gives us and our obedience demonstrates our trust in Him, and our submission to Him. We can't look at carnal examples to determine our spiritual obedience. So, what is respect anyway and what does submission look like?

---

[10] Eggerichs,E. . *Love and Respect: The Love She Most Desires, The Respect He Desperately Needs.* Detroit: Thomas Nelson Publishing, 2004.

Submission in marriage, simply put, is living a life of agreement alongside your husband. It doesn't mean that you approve of everything he does, nor does it mean that you have to do everything he says in a mindless, "Stepford Wives" manner. What submission does mean is that you are consistently and intentionally expressing your love to your husband through genuine reassurance for who he is as a man and for the value he holds as the leader of your marriage. This can be done simultaneously with other expressions of love, but not in replacement. For instance, quality time is my love language. It's the most prominent way in which I feel loved by others. When people invite me to do things or call me to talk or get coffee or go to lunch, I feel happy and valued and loved. Since I most identify with quality time, it's my natural reaction to show others love in this way, as well. I reach out to spend time because it makes me happy and therefore it's my expression of love when I want others to feel happy and valued, as well. But let's say, in my marriage, I refuse to show my love through respect and submission, but, instead, insist on sharing elaborate displays of quality time as a replacement. This isn't going to go well for my marriage.

There is no replacement for respect and no substitution for submission. God has instructed every wife to respect and submit for the mutual benefit of both the husband and the wife, as unto the Lord (Ephesians 5:21-22). This is not an isolated call only for the wife; God has instructed your husband's submission and respect under the authority of Jesus Christ for the covering of your household and the expansion of Kingdom work. This is bigger than preference, attitudes and political politeness. It's eternal and spiritual and legacy influencing. We cannot afford to make the mistake of compartmentalizing our obedience as if it applies here and not there because our obedience to the Lord is not optional – not if we claim to love Him (John 14:15).

Obedience, submission, respect and honor all point to loving well. God is love and He is always good, and His instructions are always for our good. In fact, scripture tells us that God requires our obedience "so that we might always prosper" (Deuteronomy 6:24). God delights in your marriage and He desires that it prospers because everything He has created; He has declared to be good (Genesis 1:31). God loves your marriage and He loves your husband just as much as He loves you. He knows that your husband needs the affirmation of your submission and respect to propel the mission He's placed over each of you to love well.

Ladies, submission and respect means everything to a man! By just affirming him through submission, he'll "relax [in his marriage] because he knows that even when he makes mistakes, she will be working with him to help put things right. The husband will feel secure in himself that she [his wife] will be working to minimize the consequences of life rather than trying to prove a point or reject him in some way... [her] honor of his leadership, through her submission will increase his passion for her, inciting more passion from her…" [11] I think this is such a beautiful depiction of how vital submission and respect is for a man and for a marriage. Your husband needs to know that you not only approve of him, but that you affirm him – whether he's right or whether he's wrong. God placed this dependency in his heart, and you are the only one who can ease it and affirm his value in this way. This is the other side of loving. Whether or not we think our husband is doing a good job has nothing to do with our call to respect and submit. We respect them because we trust God and our obedience to Christ will ensure our submission in marriage. It's the sure-fire way that our husband's hearts grow in full confidence in missional marriage we desire to cultivate with them (Proverbs 31:11).

Sway His Heart

"What do you think?"

It's a common question Jarrett asks me about shirt colors, vacation destinations, restaurant picks, and presidential candidates. He's not asking because he's incapable of making his own decisions, he asks me because he values my opinion. My thoughts and my words towards him, towards his interests, his growth and towards his goals, hold weight in his life. Your opinion matters to your husband, too. Opinions spoken with respect from you will cultivate an honoring

---

[11] Harley, W.F. *His Needs, Her Needs: Building an Affair-Proof Marriage.* Revell; Revised, Expanded Edition, 1986.

atmosphere of mutual trust and appreciation (1 Peter 3:7).

Our words and actions should be honoring at all times and will produce rich benefits within our marriages, our families and our relationships. Our words have power and our husbands measure themselves by the messages we proclaim about them. We have so much sway with our attitudes and in our expressions. Please do not discount the power and influence your words have in your marriage and over your husband's confidence in himself and in you.

We cannot tear our men down and expect them to feel loved or be loving. We cannot incite them through rejection and expect them to respond to us in affectionate ways. Our marriages will never thrive that way. Instead, we must be intentional about what we say and how we say it, using genuine love and not manipulation or disparaging words or attitudes. Let's not forget that love is patient and kind (1 Corinthians 13:1). This should be reflected in our words as much as in our behavior. It takes only one word to place our men on top of a mountain, or one word to crush them underneath one. Gossip, complaining, and slandering our men will never motivate them to do better or try harder. It's disrespectful and destructive. If anything, such demeaning behavior could have the potential of producing self-fulfilling prophecies within our husbands that will express themselves throughout our relationship.

"Out of the abundance of the heart, the mouth speaks"
-Matthew 12:34 (ESV)

Listen, I'm not trying to ruin your girls' night. I'm trying to detour you around catastrophe. I want you to realize the magnitude that your opinion has over your husband and I want you to use that influence with wisdom and love to spur him on to grow and become and develop into the man that God desires him to be ... the man that you desire him to be. Let's not lose focus of the goal and our mission in marriage: to love each other as Christ loves us, to spur one another to be our God given best and to share our lives with the men we have pledged our love to. This is marriage and yes, it's hard. It's a lot of selflessness, a lot of humility and a lot of forgiving and starting over again. It requires a lot of grace and a lot of intentionality. It's a lot, but you are so very capable to love well, and the rewards are unparallel if you keep the mission of marriage in mind.

Friends, your mission as a wife isn't about being catered to by a man, it's about elevating that man into his God-given destiny through the sway and influence of your love, respect and support of who he is and who he is becoming. That's a mouthful, right? But it's something to remain conscientious of because a woman who forgets the power of her influence is a woman who isn't very powerful at all.

Choose Who to Follow

What I love so much about my husband is that even when I'm unsettled and conflicted, he gives grace to me. That's one of the many things I respect so much about Jarrett - he desires to love me like Christ, whether I'm having a good day or not. He has his short comings, as all of us do, and sometimes, he does things that don't always sum up to my expectations, but it could never alter my admiration of who he is. He loves me, always chooses me and he is patient with me. I respect that and I admire the way he shows me Jesus with intention and consistency and leadership.

How often are we telling our men that we respect their leadership? How often are we cheering them on by championing them with affirmations and encouragement? My heart so desperately wants to cheer my husband on in his pursuits to love me, to love our family and to be led by the Lord. I don't always remember to do this, but when I do, it changes everything because every husband wants to love and lead well. They want to be a good covering and they want to exemplify God for our hearts and in our homes. It means a lot when we acknowledge this, and it prevents so many unnecessary problems when we control our tongues and speak what is good and true and admirable (Philippians 4:8).

Discord, disharmony, disengagement … these are all weapons of the enemy and we know his objective is to kill, steal and destroy (John 10:10). The enemy wants to wedge himself into our communication and conversations, our thought patterns and our attitudes so that he can sabotage our efforts to love well by planting disharmony. He knows if he can sow seeds of frustration, he can block our openness with one another and sometimes, this causes us to verbally and emotionally shut down. But we don't have to follow his lure. We know he is a liar and scripture tell us to resist any gateway that leads to division (Romans 16:17). The truth is that your husband doesn't want division with you. That's what the enemy wants, but we can defeat his efforts by loving and praying and blessing our husbands and refusing to follow the lies and deception that disharmony constructs. We already know we won't agree on everything, but there is a way to allow our husbands to lovingly lead us, even when we don't agree. This is accomplished when we trust God by allowing our husbands to lead us as God leads them.

I strongly believe we all truly desire to love well, but we sometimes point fingers because deep down we are struggling with respecting our husband's leadership role. Maybe we think we could make better decisions or be a better leader. Maybe we think we know more, and it's possible that we do, but shutting out, shutting down or tearing down with our words and attitudes is not the mark of good leadership. It just isn't. Speaking praiseworthy words that are authentic and true is a result of loving well. Our energy and agendas can become more focused on reconciliation and celebration and less about the concern for personal verification or position.

A man who leads is a man who must first follow. I think we can all do a better job of covering our men in prayer for the Holy Spirit to guide them. Leadership is a valuable quality, but ultimately, Ladies, God has called your husband to be the leader of your home (1 Corinthians 11:3; Ephesians 5:23) and, according to scripture, the leadership role is not up for discussion.

Facts. Period. Done.

You might not agree with me on this, but the Bible makes this very clear: God has put Christ in position to lead the Church and God has put the husband in position to lead his wife (1 Peter 3: 5-6). When we follow our men as they follow the Lord, we are bringing the Kingdom come. We are aligning our homes to represent our Heavenly home and through this obedience, we are bringing glory to God and honor within our marriages. Sometimes, it's a difficult obedience to live out. Men are different than we are, and their ways aren't always amenable to us. Sometimes, we sit back and think, "He needs to do it this way", and we may be right, but I have realized that there are times when we, as women and as wives, can be correct in our information but wrong in our timing.

Let me explain with a few examples. Who knew John the Baptist and Jesus were conceived by God's will? Women. Who told the disciples that Christ had risen from the dead? Women. Who didn't believe the women's testimony about the risen Savior and, instead, went on about their business the way they saw fit? Men. See, men don't always listen to us at first, but I truly believe that the Lord gives women early insight on many matters, not so that we can tell our men that we are right, but so that we can pray for them as God prepares their hearts for understanding in the proper timing. Our prayers help guide their clarity and the Holy Spirit, in His timing, will lead them into the fertile season to implement what you may already know. Trust God, girls! Trust Him as your husband leads you.

Listen, you will never have peace in your home if you are

intent on Boss Babe-ing your husband around. I know these are counter cultural ideas, but God has not put you in control of your home. He's given that responsibility to your husband and as long as you desire to live and love God's way, this is the order that must be respected. This by no means belittles your position, your identity as a woman, your rights or your value, but it does mean that blessing your husband and supporting him as he grows is required in a God-centered marriage. The Spirit of God leads them, they lead us, and we lift up their hearts to our ever-interceding Savior, who is working all things together for our good (Romans 8:27-28).

If you want true peace in your home, harmony in your heart and fulfilling love to continue to grow between the two of you, respect the leadership God has entrusted to your husband! I believe in this so much because I know God's way is the best way and I want to encourage you that implementing God's ways in your marriage will revitalize the both of you. God is molding our men and we should celebrate their growth instead of pointing out where they may be stumbling. Prayer is the most powerful communication of all. It's where heaven joins earth as we fall at the throne of grace and make our requests known for our men and for our families.

A praying woman is a dangerous person and God amazingly will reshape our hearts as we seek Him in prayer. More patience is what we need. More humility and graciousness and strength and wisdom. The Holy Spirit has a way of leading us in God's direction and planting our feet in the middle of His plans. Let's trust The Lord and learn to follow our men as they learn to follow Him.

What We May Have Missed

Everyone seems to have the secret sauce to what is required for lasting love, but I can confidently affirm that any measures that don't include God's divine design for loving well just isn't going to sustain long term abundance between you and your husband. Jesus is intimately interested in our love lives, just as intently as He is in our souls. Every aspect of who we are and what we go through is of great concern to the Lord so we can trust that His standards over our love is for our ultimate good. We cannot afford to miss this. We cannot overlook the impact that obedience to God through respecting our husbands is a game changer and an impact maker!

Marriage is not about you; it's about Jesus. It's about His love and His light shining through our lives as a testament to the Gospel. Showing respect to our husbands is one of the missing ingredients in so many marriages because I dare say we aren't engrossed in apply scripture into our marriages as we should be doing. It's easy to raise hands and lift voices when life is going well, but worship isn't just for Sunday morning participation; it's a lifestyle we should be living simply by obeying God's Word. He esteems marriage so highly that He uses it as a metaphor for His own relationship, through Salvation, with all Believers (Hosea 2:20; Revelation 19:17). He declares that marriage must be held in honor among all (Hebrews 13:4), and that "all" includes wives. Respecting our husbands isn't simultaneous with us losing respect for ourselves, but it is advantageous to our marriages when we trust God by obeying His word. Withholding respect might make you feel strong in the inconsistent moment, but it will make a man feel weak in the long run, and one thing I know is that a man who feels weak is a man who won't try.

Men crave environments where they receive recognition and respect and they will soar to new heights synonymous with your perception, and your praise of who they are and the efforts they are making. No husband wants to come home to a disrespectful wife – a wife who is always annoyed with him; a wife who grunts and complains; a wife who is pushy and criticizing and rarely cheers him on; a wife who is manipulative or indifferent. Eventually, men will begin to avoid such environments and retreat to atmospheres where they feel like a winner. If he's only feeling respected at work, he'll pour himself into his profession. If he only finds it on the court or on the golf course, that's where he'll go. If he's not feeling respected at home, that's where he won't go. He'll find other means to fill that void and that is a slippery slope into the enemy's camp. If the enemy can separate the two of you spatially, he'll try to separate the two of you emotionally and spiritually. I don't think that's a risk any wife wants to take. We must be mindful that our actions are expressing accurate messages because a man will interpret what you show him just as effectively as what you say to him.

In his book, *Love and Respect*, Emerson Eggerichs makes this statement, "love [emotionally] is vital, especially for the wife, but what we have missed is the husband's need for respect."[12] Men are wired to seek affection through respect because men and women were created differently. Equal in value; different in disposition (Genesis 5:2). Until we understand that what fuels us may not necessarily fuel our men, we will find ourselves out of step with what most secures their hearts in our love for them. This is why the Bible differentiates what a wife needs, and what a husband needs:

"However, let each one of you love his wife as himself, and let the wife see that she respects her husband."
— Ephesians 5:33 (ESV)

A woman who desires to love well will take note of this. Our husbands need our respect as badly as we need their attention and affection. We want our men to have full confidence in us and to be excited to come home to us. We want our men to be drawn to us and to be satisfied by us. A woman of noble character who desires God's presence in her home and in her heart knows that loving her husband well is a form of worship to the Lord and a valuable treasure to her man and thus, produces great rewards within her marriage. This is what respecting our husbands is all about. It's not about doing what we're told or about staying in place and in line. That's not love, and our husbands have been commanded (not

---

[12] Eggerichs, E. *Love and Respect: The love she most desires, the respect he desperately needs.* Thomas Nelson, 2004.

asked) to love us the exact same way that Christ loves the church. Jesus gave up His all for the church, sacrificed everything and won it all back for the church – His bride. This is how our husbands are told to love us. In the same measure, we have been commanded to respect him; not as if respect is a reward we bequeath in exchange for our approval, but we submit our respect to our husbands out of obedience to the Lord and love for our men. Remember, blessings always proceed obedience and we will surely receive favor in our marriages when we resolve to love as God designed.

I find this balance incredible! The command is to the men first: Love your wives. Honor your wives. Protect, guard, lead and defend your wives. Doesn't that just naturally inspire you to extend respect? And as we extend our respect to our husbands, the beauty is that this obedience on our part will naturally and spiritually compel them to respond in loving us more deeply. This truly takes my breath away! It makes me think about my newfound love of plants. I currently have about ten house plants that I'm learning to care for and I'm learning so much about the benefits of keeping living plants in my home. Not only are they gorgeous, but they are beneficial to our health in many ways, particularly through filtering the air that we breathe. My carbon dioxide benefits the plant and I benefit from the plant's release of oxygen. The plant doesn't give me oxygen because I deserve it – it just does what it was created to do. I don't give the plant carbon dioxide because it deserves it. It just naturally gets released from my body and profits the plant, the way it was intended to do. Love and respect have the same results in marriage.

It's not a reward, it's a response and the results produce full bloom growth, maturity and pleasures for each of us in our unions. Obedience to do this should be our joy because we realize the reward in it.

It's clear that respect is missing in many marriages, but it doesn't have to be a missing piece in yours. Respecting your husband is not misogynistic as society tries to lecture. It's not belittling, authoritarian or subservient. It's life giving and will enhance a marriage from good to great, barely to beautiful, dwindling to thriving. This is God's plan because He made men and women different. We are equal in our value, but different in our needs. We as women want the sweet gestures and the exchange of deep feelings and tender moments. We know that men aren't wired quite like that because they aren't like us so therefore, they need something different than we do. They need a pat on the back. They need the sense that they are heroic to us. They need to be upheld and championed and applauded. This is what respect looks like and in a man's world, it's synonymous with our desire to be adored.

God designed men this way, so loving our husbands in godly ways includes respecting them. The root of this is in fact love. See, as we grow to love them, we will grow to respect them. Respect is produced through our love. The more we chose to love our husbands, the greater our respect for them will grow and the more we respect them, the more their love for us will develop as a result. This takes us back to previous chapters where we discussed that love is a choice. If we have the power to choose to love our husbands, then we also have the power to choose to respect them. This isn't robotic obedience; it's a genuine response to the love and trust we have for them and the trust we have in the Lord. This realization makes respecting our men a joy and a delight and is one of the key markers of a flourishing marriage that we all desire to have.

So, let me ask you a real question. The women who are not practicing respect for their husbands, who are dismissive and indifferent – do they have thriving marriages that you want to immolate? Odds are, they don't. Why? Because where there is disrespect, there is disharmony.

Here is the Recipe

What I am learning is exactly what we've been discussing: respecting and submission is a result of loving them well. As we love them, our respect will unfold in three ways: we will begin to celebrate who they are becoming, cover their hearts as they learn to lead us and when differences arise, we entrust them to the Lord. That's the submission part – not to blaze past them in annoyance or defiance, but to affirm them as we believe in them and pray for them.

There have been many occurrences in my marriage where I have struggled to submit under Jarrett. He lives life much slower than I prefer and I sometimes feel he gets too comfortable in a particular area or unmotivated in others. He's got a keen sense for business and a natural confidence with people, but there have been times where I felt his self-assurance wasn't where I knew it could be.

After talks with my Mother about my frustrations and confusions, she taught me that men respond well when we speak futuristically. Instead of trying to have motivational talks with him about where I think he needs to grow or how I wish he'd be more conscientious, I've learned to thank him for things he's yet to do and I've learned to cheer him in achievements he's yet to accomplish. For example, I will often tell him how excited I am to meet 35-year-old Jarrett; implying that I see greatness in his future. When he comes home with ideas for work, I've made it a point to tell him that there is nothing he can't do and that I'll be ready with my best dress on when the results come in. Championing him in this way has truly built his confidence in himself and in me. It makes him feel respected, supported and deeply loved. He's more enthusiastic to share his ideas and ask my opinions because he knows there will be encouragement in what he'll hear from me, even if my response doesn't reflect complete approval. I don't have to agree with him on everything … and I don't. Sometimes, I just want to shake my head and go shopping, but in spite of it all, I do believe in him and he knows it!

When situations arise that I am hesitant for him to pursue, I express my opinions and then I give it to the Lord. Sometimes, I'll just grab his hand right there in the parking lot or in the kitchen and pray for him on the spot. In our seven years of love, I have learned how important it is to cover his heart in prayer and ask for guidance, assurance and peace as I cheer him on. I can't declare that I do this every single time, but when I do remember to pause to cheer Jarrett and trust God, the Lord always works things out.

While Jarrett and I were still dating, we both expressed an interest in pursuing our Master's degrees. This was the plan that I held tightly to and I was swift to begin my program. Two years after we were married, I had completed my degree, but he hadn't applied yet. I was completely frustrated, and I couldn't understand what his hesitation was. We were soon pregnant with our first daughter and I was getting uneasy. I'd bring it up, constantly, which annoyed him and furthered my frustrations. We certainly had a fair share of arguments over it, and, to my dismay, Jarrett expressed to me that I was being pushy and forceful. I felt so confused and devastated and I didn't know what to do. Nothing I said seemed to be motivating him to apply. It bewildered me and I began to act out my annoyance in disrespectful ways. I'm so ashamed to admit this, but I became short spoken, critical and impatient with him. I knew his dreams required that he achieve that degree and I truly believe in all of his dreams. Why wouldn't he budge? How could I motivate him to do what I knew he needed to do?

One day, I sat with my Mother outside in her garden and I just spilled it all out to her. I told her how I felt like Jarrett was undermining his own potential and that I was afraid that if he didn't begin his studies now, he may never find the time after our child was born. I felt that putting off this degree was selfish and could prevent our family from financially advancing. I told my mom that I was afraid that he may be settling, and I told her that I felt like Jarrett wasn't listening to me and that he didn't care. I just went on and on and I sat there sobbing. I was so tired of feeling powerless and uninfluential. I was so exhausted from our disagreements on the matter. I just didn't know what to do. Of course, my Mother listened quietly the whole time, like mothers often do. She didn't say one word until I was finished. She must have been waiting for me to sob my last and when I finally fell silent, she said something that I will never forget. Frances Coleman looked at me in that sweet mom way of hers and said the most profound thing to me.

"Trina", she said, "only God can make Jarrett see what Jarrett cannot see."

Mind blown!

I want to pass along the same advice and encouragement to you. Honey, only God can show your man what he cannot see. Fussing, arguing and nagging, pushing, complaining, criticizing … none of that is going to change your husband because none of that is respectful. Just love him. Just remind him of how much you believe in his dreams. Remind him of all the greatness you want to achieve with him. Celebrate who he is and who he is becoming. That's the recipe for respect. You cannot change him. That's God's job, so leave it in His hands. Pray for your husband and rely on God to change his heart and mind in whatever area you're concerned about. That's exactly what I decided to do. I took my Mother's advice to tell Jesus all about it. I poured out all my concerns and fears and uncertainties and shared Jarrett's dreams with the Lord and my desire to see those dreams come into existence. Jarrett didn't suddenly apply the next hour, but what ended up happening was that God began to change me. He started showing me that He was in control and He took away my fears and uncertainties that I was harboring. He showed me that He was our sustainer and that a degree could not cover us the way His love can.

Slowly, the Lord starting shining lights on areas I was unaware of. There were early mornings where I would stumble upon Jarrett quietly reading his Bible in the kitchen, taking notes and praying over our family. I had no idea he had been doing this all along. God began to open my eyes to His work in Jarrett's life and He showed me that Jarrett was seeking after His will, so I just needed to trust God's process and be patient. That season taught me what respectful love really meant. I was still bothered by the situation, but I was no longer consumed by it. I stopped nagging Jarrett about his degree and the time once spent on arguing was soon replaced with baby day-dreaming and joyful anticipation of our daughter. The lack of tension truly allowed us to bond in deeper ways as we prepared for parenthood. It was such a blessing and we truly needed such peace and harmony in that particular season because the experience of pregnancy took a toll on me, health wise. I couldn't imagine going through that while being at odds with my husband. God is faithful and He is the One putting things in place and in order.

Looking back, I'm so thankful for my Mother's advice and even more grateful that the Lord gave me the wisdom to implement it. My marriage grew so rich with the lack of constant arguing and tension. God had answered my prayers and showed me that He was moving in ways I didn't realize we needed in our marriage. He showed me that Jarrett needed my affirmation and I truly saw him grow as a person, as a husband and as a professional. Two months before Kailyn was born, we received an acceptance letter in the mail from his university of study, along with a scholarship from Jarrett's company and boy, did we celebrate! Jarrett finished his MBA program right before Kailyn's second birthday and I couldn't have been prouder of him!

It's in our waiting that we can trust God and it's in our loving that we can respect our husbands and watch God do what only God can do. He is the only One who can change hearts and make all things right (Romans 8:28). This is why we must invite the Lord into our homes and into our hearts, so that God can be God. He is in control, not you. He has, however, called you to the mission of loving your husband and He has equipped you with feminine finesse to get the job done. This is just as intellectual as it is sexual because as we learn our husbands, we learn how to support him in ways that are meaningful to him, thus using our wifely influence to produce productive results through our love, submission and respect. This is what the Bible refers to when it calls a wife a helpmate (Genesis 2:18) and this is why the Bibles teaches that a woman was made for and from a man (1 Corinthians 11:8-9).

God saw to it that man shouldn't be alone (Genesis 2:18). The creation of woman was the Lord's supreme idea. In fact, scripture tells us that it wasn't Adam that asked for a helpmate; it was God who recognized that man needed one. Doesn't that just make you smile? Our husbands truly do need us, and they need our support and our respect. They need our prayers, just as we need them to pray for us.

Behind every good man is a great woman. It's cliché, but it's true! Great women know how to exert their influence and address their men in ways that do not undermine them or disrespect them. There's an art to this and it requires wisdom beyond magazine articles. It requires God's Word and God's voice to know how to support our men in meaningful ways and to truly be the helpmate the Lord has entrusted us to be. The enemy wants to distract you with perceived weakness in your husband, but the Lord is at work in each of you and He desires that you turn your attention to the ways that He is molding your husband and developing him as the leader and head of your home (Ephesians 5:23). This is not advocating the notion that we as women should be seen and not heard. I'm not for that at all. God has blessed you with a brain and valuable opinions. You have just as many rights and freedoms in Christ as any man. So, hear my heart in what I am encouraging you with. I'm not saying that support and respect requires you to lay low or keep quiet. No one gets helped if we refuse to speak. There is no sin or shame to sharing your thoughts, concerns and conflicting feelings if your husband makes decisions that you are uneasy about. But respecting your husband means loving your husband, even when you disagree, knowing that the Lord will take care of everything.

I truly want us all to develop into wives who love well and

who speak the truth, in love, while also entrusting the Lord with the outcome. Remember, it's the Spirit who makes truth clear (John 16:13). We cannot make our husbands see our point of view and we cannot force them to agree with our perspective by disrespecting them. This will only prevent us from the honor and opportunity to speak into their lives. Instead, we can go to the Lord in prayer for whatever changes are necessary for the sake of our marriage because God does care. There are places in your husband's heart that you cannot reach, but God can, and He will if you invite Him to do so.

After this, we wait. We pray and we wait. We read our Bibles and pray and wait because it takes time. We need time to change and so do our husbands. God doesn't always work instantly. Our prayers aren't always answered immediately, but every prayer will always receive an answer. God is at work and He is our good Father who enjoys responding to us. In one of three ways, the Lord will always answer us with either "Yes", "No" or "Not now". The "Yes" is what we desire, but sometimes it's the "No" that is best for us. "Not now" can be its own challenge, as we wait like little girls in the back seat of a car, intrigued by the journey, though uncertain of the destination. But God knows exactly where He is taking us, and He uses time to teach us and to prepare us.

As we wait, grace is made available because mistakes may arise in each of us. We're imperfect people, after all, so we need to rely on the Lord, and we need to implement encouragement, love and respect towards one another. Such love will cover issues that may surface in between our prayers and our answers. Grace will also prevent us from the urge to point out where our men may not be measuring up to our expectations. This can be so tough, but God is greater, and He is using every instance and every moment, every situation and every circumstances for the good of our marriages and the glory of His name!

Women who practice the godly principle of respecting their husbands understand that this is a spiritual support. As they learn to lead us in deeper and fuller love and become all that God has called them to be, the grace of your respect and the patience of your love will be an anchor to them and a safe place for them. Remember, you two are a team. A team doesn't drag along its members through force or ultimatums; it motivates and encourages and champions every member on to triumph! A man will become his greatest and fullest self in a marriage where he feels celebrated and respected. So, have the conversations, speak your mind, in love, seek ways to celebrate him and walk alongside him as God directs your marriage. Instead of reminding him of who he isn't, declare over him who he will be and then cover it all in prayer. This is respect. This is love. It demonstrates that you see greater and abundant things in your husband, and this will produce a determination within him to prove you right.

Reflection

Our culture teaches that a woman has the right to choose whether or not her husband deserves her respect. How does the Biblical relationship between love and respect counteract that idea?

<u>Scriptures for Your Soul</u>

"Husbands, love your wives, as Christ loved the church and gave himself up for her… In the same way husbands should love their wives as their own bodies. He who loves his wife loves himself. For no one ever hated his own flesh, but nourishes and cherishes it, just as Christ does the church, because we are members of his body. "Therefore, a man shall leave his father and mother and hold fast to his wife, and the two shall become one flesh." … let each one of you love his wife as himself, and let the wife see that she respects her husband."

-Ephesians 5: 25-33

CHAPTER 6

LOVE WHO HE LOVES

I believe that family is very important to most of us, if not all of us. True, we may not all have the Full House TV family, but we love the people who belong to us, no matter the history or varying lifestyles. But what about your husband's family? Are they as easy to love, flaws and all, as your own imperfect family? According to Psychology Today, the answer is not likely. A study conducted on over 700 marriages who had been married for under 10 years revealed that in-law clash was a common occurrence for conflict in marriage. [13] These results weren't limited to race or ethnicity, socio-economic status, education or how much in love the married couple were.

In-laws (or out-laws) have a strange influence over us and over our marriages. It's not shocking when married couples collide

---

[13] Greif, G. (2020, January 03). Daughters-in-Law and Mothers-in-Law: Boundary Ambiguity. Retrieved March 06, 2020, from https://www.psychologytoday.com/us/blog/buddy-system/202001/daughters-in-law-and-mothers-in-law-boundary-ambiguity

with one another's families because, in spite of commonalities we may have with our husbands, there may be people within the ext3ending family that you just won't be able to get away from or get along with. He may have friends that might not be the best influence and family that can be quite arduous. He may have an ex that's not agreeable or have co-workers that aren't at his maturity level; weather they are friends or family, it can be quite tough! Even though I personally know many women who've been blessed to inherit harmonious and loving in-laws and formed secure and respectful relationships with them, I know this is not everyone's experience. So, what do we do with the people who love our husbands, but can't seem to get along with us? How do we handle conflict with people who aren't interested in understanding or accepting us in their family?

Recently, I spent an afternoon chatting with some sweet friends about this very issue. We talked about our own experiences, as well as the experiences of our mothers, our sister's experiences with their husband's family, other friends, cousins, co-workers ... on and on, and it occurred to me that the conflict I have often endured within my own in-law relationships aren't unique. Many women face disharmony with someone on their husband's side of the family; not necessarily because of any fault of their own, but simply because of limited perspectives and perceptions. Unless any of us take the time to extend relationship through intentional understanding and acceptance, the soil for conflict is made ripe and ready. Though disparaging, the point of all conflict is to distract us from loving well and sadly, many of us fall prey to the distraction instead of victorious over it.

Family is a gift, but it's also a challenge meant to provide us the opportunity to live out our love in selfless ways. It's not always going to be the reception, ladies. Sometimes, our inherited families make us regret our decision for marriage all together, but you have the victory in Christ's love to love who your husband loves in authentic and spiritual ways, no matter what they've done to you or said about you. Sitting across the table, gleaning from friends who've been married for 9 years, 12 years and even 14 years, my conflicted heart was eased and reassured and left me more inspired to discover ways to love everyone that I am connected to. I know your heart desires the same. Sometimes, however, it just doesn't seem natural or possible.

<u>The Challenge</u>

As I have navigated through the beginnings of my marriage, emotional strain within the family relationships I married into have been challenging, to say the very least. There have been some hopeful moments, for sure, but there have also been some extremely difficult seasons that have taken huge blows on me, personally. Feeling attacked is never fun and being out right rejected takes its toll. I've endured a lot in my seven years of marriage, and it has driven me to my knees in tearful prayers and pleading with the Lord for direction, and for help.

On one particular occasion, as I heaved painful prayers to Jesus, I found myself literally pounding my fists in frustration, recounting all the unkindness that I'd experienced from certain in-laws. I vulnerably told the Lord that it wasn't fair and that I didn't deserve the mistreatment, the gossip, the name calling or the rejection. I reminded God of how tender hearted I am and how I just didn't understand why He would place me in a family who didn't accept me for who He created me to be. Girl, I went in! I had such a spiritual pity party, right there in the car, crying about my feelings and my efforts and my perspective and my disappointment. It was an utterly selfish moment, but just like a good Father, the Lord gently revealed to me that I wasn't called to be loved by everyone; I was called to be loving towards everyone. With such a still, small voice in my heart, my Creator and my Redeemer, who made the intricate parts of my heart and emotions, reassured me that His love was enough.

Friends, not everyone is going to like us, and we have to be ok with that. The value of our lives is not based on the opinions that others impose on us. Opinions are never based in truth, but rather perspective and perception are always biased. Instead, we must hold tight to what Jesus declares over us: that we are His chosen treasure, His good works, His daughters and His friends (Colossians 3:12; Ephesians 2:10; Galatians 3:26; John 15:15). Since we have already been justified by Christ, we don't need to prove ourselves to anyone. Jesus has already proven our value on Calvary. He has proven His love for us on the cross and it's the power of His love that propels us to love others in powerful ways, even those whom we feel don't deserve it. We have to surrender the pain and every offense to Him. It's not easy at all, but when we surrender those spaces that feel ruined and broken, He will capture the situations that we cannot control.

Surrender can be such a challenge because we picture it like waving a white flag and giving in to the villain of our stories. But remember, people are not our enemy. We aren't waring against flesh and blood (Ephesians 6:12). Our fight is with the problem produced by unloving choices – the sin of unkindness enacted upon out of rebellion of God's love. Disharmony is the deception of the enemy and people, even in our families, are being deceived. But our obedience to sharing the love of Christ shines light in all darkness. We can entrust the Lord to clean out all bitterness so that we do not become the reflection of pain, but rather become the transformation of it. What better way to share the Gospel than to love those who oppose us? Isn't this what Christ did for us?

Loving our husband's loved ones can be challenging from time to time, but it is a form of loving him and it's a form of loving God. Once this becomes the disposition in which we make our decisions, we can operate by extending grace for the difficult and love for the undeserving. We can make a place and space for anyone in our extended circles even if they have not done the same for us, because it's not about us. It's about Jesus. His love is always challenging us to go beyond and to be transformed. It's an act of trust and faith and courage and it's the work of the Holy Spirit to love beyond our limitations, seventy times seven and time again (Matthew 18:22). The cowardly way is to reject what's difficult by refusing to try. Love requires effort. Love requires action. The quality of your love if revealed by your efforts and actions, but the lack of love is represented by the absence of it. There is no way around it. So, in order to love well, we must begin by doing well. We must submit our feelings to Jesus and choose to do what is right; no matter what it looks like, no matter how it feels or who's watching or how they respond. That's the challenge of loving well.

Crying to Jesus in the car, I wiped away snot and tears from my face and a very challenging question echoed in my heart: Am I willing to love those who God loves or am I only interested in loving those who love me? The challenge of this question is one we all should be considering and answering for ourselves when it comes to marriage and family relationships. Our response will always reflect what's in our heart.

"This is how everyone will recognize that you are my disciples—when they see the love you have for each other."
-John 13:35 (NLT)

People will recognize our love for God by the way we love them. On the flip side, they will recognize our lack of love for the Lord if we choose to be unloving. That's the deal: those who are unloving don't have God's love. That's not my opinion; it's scripture (1 John 4:20). We cannot claim love for God while mistreating people who are loved by God. It's a challenge sometimes, for sure, but understand that every single connection and relationship in your life is God's strategic invitation for His love and light to shine through you. His love is so righteous, and He calls us to love righteously – no exceptions. In ourselves, it's not always possible, but through His Spirit, it always is.

Loving like Jesus is challenging. Loving people outside of our home in unconditional ways isn't always easy, but "the one who does what is right is righteous, just as He is righteous … the one who does not do what is right is not God's child, nor is anyone who does not love their brother or sister" (1 John 3:7-8; 10). Your family, whether the one you were born to or the one that you married into, are a collection of your brothers and sisters. They are people, loved by God and made in His image. We must always remind ourselves of this. You and your husband are not an island; you never were, and you never will be. From the day each of you were born, there were people connected to you and the marriage that linked your lives also connected you to the lives of those who have formulated and shaped who you are and who your husband is. They don't just dissolve into the backgrounds of our marriages. They are present and they have value. Some of them will struggle with your new roles as an independent family, yet the calling and the challenge to love well remains.

I know all of us desire family, it's why we got married. Family is such a beautiful blessing. Each member holds a place and worth. The same goes with friendships. These are people who have shaped us, cheered us on, supported us and loved us. Naturally, we want everyone to get along and to love our lovers with eager acceptance and understanding, just as we do. Unfortunately, it's not always as natural of a transition as we'd like this to be. There may be times when outside actions and opinions from family or friends negatively affect you in some way. It's bound to happen, because, as my Father always says, "Where there are people, there are problems". You see, each person in your husband's life, whether they get along with you or not, loves him, and each feel a degree of entitlement to him. They may not see you the same way, therefore, they may not treat you the same way. This could be in unintentional ways due to family cultures, differences and personalities, or it could be deliberate. Either way, it can be quite hurtful, but our calling and challenge is to love, regardless.

<u>Family Frustrations</u>

When we enter into a new family, we are entering into an established community of people who have their own stories, their own traditions, habits and perspectives that we may not understand or recognize right away. The same is true for people in your life. Your husband might be oblivious to the social norms and constructs of your family's lifestyle and nuances. He may not be aware of what is and is not considered acceptable to do or say. This is why one of my number one suggestion is to spend extensive time with each other's families during your dating season. It's important to glimpse a picture of who you will be connecting yourself with, as well as an opportunity for your family to get to know your future spouse. There are so many "Ahh Ha" moments that can come from forming relationships before the wedding day, however, even these measures aren't a guarantor. Merging two lives and two families isn't always a seamless process. We're all learning here, but not everyone will have patience or grace to extend over our new unions or differing lifestyles. Should this happen, it could cause a lot of frustrations, tension and hurt.

Extended family disfunction is one of the major key factors in marital separation and divorce[14]. But this doesn't have to be our story. Instead, we can strengthen our unions and protect our hearts from offense by choosing to intentionally love those who our husbands love, while constructing margins that protect our hearts and our homes. Our marriages do not have to crumble under the stress of any circling clashes or misunderstandings. We don't have to be passive in our approach, but we do need to seek out every opportunity to usher in unity and harmony where possible (Colossians 3:13). This is an act of compassion, empathy and inclusion. We must treat people the way we want to be treated, not in the way that they may be treating us.

I know family can be frustrating, and friendships that are forced upon us can be difficult to navigate sometimes, but not impossible, and I want to encourage you to try, just as I am

---

[14] Apter, T. (2009, August 11). In-law Conflict and Troubled Marriages. Retrieved April 05, 2020, from
https://www.psychologytoday.com/us/blog/domestic-intelligence/200908/in-law-conflict-and-troubled-marriages

encouraging myself to do the same. It begins with keeping in mind that your husband lived an entirely different life before you were in it. He had relationships and deep bonds with other people before you became his wife. They deserve your consideration simply because of the value they hold in your husband's life. It's not always easy, but your love and devotion for him will become more evident and flourish greatly if you learn to love who he loves.

A Little Kindness

A study done by Lesley University concluded that social cognitive formation (or personality) is "the adaptation and assimilation of observed behaviors".[15] Personality, therefore, is composed of a collection of experiences which an individual interprets and then acts upon in order to help express their unique perspective of their existence. So, basically, a person's personality is a reflection of their familiarities, while behavior is what one chooses to do. What does any of this have to do with how we are treated by our in-laws, or by any other person for that matter? Well, people treat you the way they've been treated. But Jesus teaches us a new way of handling people. Rather than respond to people the way we've been responded to, He commands us to reverse our natural inclinations in one very profound sentence.

---

[15] Williard, G. (2019). The Science of Personality Development. Retrieved March 18, 2020, from https://lesley.edu/article/personality-development

"Do to others whatever you would like them to do to you."
-Matthew 7:12 (ESV)

As I was reading various articles on human behavior for this portion of our book, that scripture kept ringing out to me. No wonder Jesus taught it. If, by nature, we are all prone to treat others the way we have been treated, it's a completely counter cultural notion to flip our innate dispositions around and focus on treating others the way we'd like to be treated, instead; being proactive rather than reactive. It takes a transformation within our spirits to show grace in replace of rejection or to reach out instead of withholding. It's easier to do it when we see the personal benefit of it, such as with a child or with a sibling, but it gets complicated very quickly when we're asked to do this with everyone. Yet this is what Jesus requires us to do and we have no excuse to do it if His love flows through us. The scripture tells us that we can do all things through Christ (Philippians 4:13); that includes loving the difficult people in our lives by just showing them a little kindness.

Loving well, at times, will go against everything that seems natural to us, particularly when we are being asked to be kind to those who are unkind and to be loving to those who are unloving (Matthew 5:44). The love we have for our spouse won't change one another's family members any more than we can choose who they are. Extended family and close-knit friendships are often part of the package of marriage that we may not have considered beforehand. Yes, our covenant is with our husbands, but our life as a married couple will include other people. As we continue to seek ways to do what is right when it comes to loving through personality conflicts and differences, one thing is for sure, kindness is always the loving thing to do.

Never forget that the Lord sits high and looks low. He knows every intention and every motive, and He will judge us all according to every choice we make and every single word we think or speak (Matthew 12:36). A woman who desires to love well does so as unto the Lord, not as unto the person. One day, we will all stand before our holy and righteous God who will not see our emotions as an excuse for unkindness. He will reward those who persist under trials (James 1:12) and will bless those who honor Him (1 Samuel 2:30). In my situation, I have come to the conclusion that loving who my husband loves is loving who God also loves. I have been called to be salt and light. You have been called to be the same. You don't have to like the behavior, but keep in mind that kindness is not a reward. Jesus isn't asking us to reward people, He's asking us to be kind to people. So, go higher, because, for a child of God, unkindness is beneath you. Lay your wounded ego, your disappointments, your rage, offense and your pride at the foot of the cross. Clinging to such things will prevent you from loving well. Instead, give hope, extend invitations, offer encouragement and share the love of Christ with whomever has hurt you. This is what it means to shine your light and it will always point to Jesus! He is your banner, your anchor and your rock (Song of Solomon 2:4; Hebrews 6:19; 1 Peter 2:6). He placed you in the family you are in for a reason. He intended you to become that sister-in-law, that daughter-in-law, that cousin, that aunt, that friend. He aligned your life to marry into that family and He is entrusting you to love who He loves. Trust His plan for your life. His love and kindness will never put you to shame.

Unmet Expectations

When I married Jarrett, it involved inheriting an enormous family that all lived in the same small town: siblings, parents, cousins, aunts, uncles, kin folk. Some of them live across the street from one another. They celebrate birthdays all together, holidays all together, vacations all together and they just invite themselves over unscheduled- all together! There's nothing wrong with this, but it wasn't what I was used to with my family. It's not how I grew up. My family environment was quite different. Growing up, it was just my parents, my brother and myself in Charlotte, North Carolina. Our family interactions involved just the four of us, and my upbringing was very intimate and very close knit, filled with one-on-one time and intimate conversations. We enjoy traveling and fishing, live music, theatre and good cuisine, but we did those things together because my extended family are sprinkled throughout different parts of the country. We would visit our loved ones a few times a year, but I didn't grow up down the street from my cousins. I never had aunts and uncles at my birthday parties or experienced extended family on a daily basis. I just wasn't accustomed to the dynamics of Jarrett's family culture that, perhaps, was the assumption. The same is true on my side of things. I expected to have deep and heartfelt conversations with the women in the family and grow close in friendship. I expected to be accepted simply because I loved Jarrett, and I thought my good intentions would be obvious to all. This, however, wasn't the case with every member of his family. There were times where I felt utterly misunderstood and I just didn't know what to do. It was difficult, and to be honest, it still is. I assumed blending into the family would be natural, but sometimes it's not so simple.

According to author and pastor, Dr. Gary Chapman, "Just as it takes time to build other close relationships, gaining acceptance into a family doesn't happen instantly."[16] In his book, *"Things I Wish I'd Known Before We Got Married"*, Dr. Chapman expounds upon the reality that unmet expectations contribute to misunderstandings which arise profusely within the first three to five years of marriage. He goes on to share that expectations derive from assumptions. Many assumptions turn into offense when they are unmet. This is what leads us into conflict: unwillingness to part with expectations or to resolve misunderstandings. A lack of harmony can easily create offended hearts and if we are not careful, relationships can be destroyed in irreversible ways. I don't want this for any of us; I want greater for us all because I know that love, no matter the outcome, is the greatest of all things (1 Corinthians 13:13).

Jarrett and I are still in our beginning season of love and

---

[16] Chapman, G. D. *Things I Wish I'd Known Before We Got Married.* Chicago: Northfield Publishing, 2010.

marriage, and in spite of all that we have overcome, we still have "promises to keep and miles to go before we sleep", as spoken by the great Robert Frost.[17] But life is not a poem. Life is not always tidy, with predictable repetitions, pretty little lines and an impressive ending. Sometimes, the lives connected to our marriages can feel like a huge imposition on us and deflate our well-intended expectations. It's easy to reject people, deny our responsibilities and to refuse to sit at the table and resolve the conflicts, but that is not love. Instead, we can ask the Lord for more grace to accept people for who they are and love them where they are, rather than focus on unmet the disparagement of unmet expectations.

Pressing Through the Persecution

Faith's mother-in-law disrespects her parenting choices, particularly when it comes to nutrition. She gives the kids treats that Faith is unapproving of and tells Faith she is too extreme.

Nicole's husband has a child-hood friend who swears around her sons. She and her husband have addressed this with him, but the friend thinks it's funny and feels Nicole is too serious.

---

[17] Allen, G. W., Rideout, W. B., & Robinson, J. K.. *American Poetry*. New York: Harper & Row, 1960.

Jade is frustrated with her future sisters-in-laws. They have said some sarcastic things about her wedding plans and haven't seemed very interested in formulating a cordial relationship with her.

Tara's in-laws were very distant with her until she had her daughter and now their overwhelming involvement and unwanted "help" feels like an imposition.

Melissa is trying to navigate her life as a Stepmother. It's been a difficult transition and her husband's ex hasn't been very pleasant or understanding of her new relationship with the kids.

You may not relate to the examples I've included, but you can insert your own example for reference purposes. Who has caused you discomfort? Who has been difficult to love? It's ok to admit it, even if only to yourself. This in no way criminalizes you, but admitting conflict will prepare you for resolution, even if it's only within yourself.

Whatever the tension or the awkward conflict, I get it. Seriously, I do get it. I get how uncomfortable it can be to deal with difficult people, but what the Lord has been teaching me, through my failures and feelings of distress when it comes to dealing with conflict in my marriage, is that the loving thing to do is to simply love, because people who are loving chose to love people. It's as simple as that.

"Pray for those who persecute you, that you may be children of your Father in heaven … If you love those who love you, what reward will you get? Are not even the pagans doing that? And if you greet only your own people, what are you doing more than others?"
– Matthew 5:44-47 (NLT)

Persecution is emotional distress caused by someone who has unjustly treated or offended you without remorse. I think, if we are honest, we desire justice and vengeance for unfair treatment, but Christ calls us to love those who persecute us, and I believe, in the depths of your heart, this is what you want to do; this is who you want to be, so be that person. Be that woman!

It's so imperative to our witness that we learn to release people with kindness, rather than throw them away in anger. Rejecting people who have rejected us doesn't show the love of Christ. Jesus tells us not to resist the ones who have wronged us (Matthew 5: 38). Instead, we are commanded to repay no one with evil and to do good to everyone (1 Thessalonians 5:15). We can be obedient in this task while still implementing grace and space around our hearts in pursuit of loving well. Release, but don't reject. Include, but don't force. Sometimes, this feels like we've been called to recompense those who've insulted us, but scripture declares that our kindness in place of payback is actually a form of penalty on the wrong doer and a reward for the righteous (Proverbs 25:22)! Crazy, I know, but God uses our kindness towards unkindness to humble others and elevate Himself in our lives.

Every decision we make to forgive, to extend peace, to give grace and to show kindness, in spite of the damage and the difficulties, not only glorifies God, but it also radiates love within your marriage and results in favor from the Lord! Remember, in Christ, you are seated in Heavenly places and this requires that you conduct yourself in Heavenly ways. I know it's so very tough, but in our weaknesses Christ's love is made strong (2 Corinthians 12:9). Listen, I know it's not easy, but my cheer for us all is to just keep loving. There is nothing more beautiful than a woman who cares for others, reaches out and offers grace over offense and extends opportunities to have healing conversations and begin again. This is a pure heart and there is nothing more powerful or brave. The world displays different responses, but we are not of this world (John 15: 18-19). Our weapons are hope, peace and love – it's something that no one can take away from us, because it was placed within us by the Lord. We don't have to explode or verbally defecate on others as an outlet for our personal frustrations or emotional instabilities. That is not strength, it's a lack of self-control. It's immature, it's unproductive and it's ugly. You are better than that. You are a woman of royal disposition, covered by your Savior and marked by the triumph of His love! Remember, we must live by the freedom of the Spirit which brings life (2 Corinthians 3:6), not the flesh which brings death by way of sin (James 1:15). Afterall, it's sin that causes dysfunction and disharmony. It's sin that creates separation and unkindness. We don't win by implementing sin. We win by the love of Christ.

"Let all bitterness and wrath and anger and clamour and slander be put away from you, along with all malice. Be kind to one another, tender-hearted, forgiving one another, as God in Christ forgave you."
-Ephesians 4:31-32 (NIV)

We cannot behave like those who have hurt us and expect the abundance of God in our lives. We can choose, instead, to respond like Jesus! I know it can be difficult. I know it's not what you deserve, but your husband does deserve your effort to love his loved ones. He didn't choose them any more than you did, and truth be told, he's just as irritated with them as you are for treating his wife, whom he did choose, with disregard. I promise, you are not the only one hurting. Think about it: he brought you into his family with expectations that you would be welcomed and loved. Their mistreatment of you is disrespect towards him. So, consider his disappointment when you are not valued the way he knows you should be. It's unfortunate, but he has no control over the choices that his family or friends make. He's caught in the middle and I promise you, he isn't having any fun. He's frustrated, too. He's tired, too. He's feeling disrespected by them, too. He wants harmony for you, and he wants harmony for himself. You're in this together, please don't lose sight of that.

If I am to be honest, there have been moments when I didn't realize the hurt my husband was carrying over the disharmony that I was experiencing with some of his family members. He did what he could to bring peace and understanding, but you can't control people. All you can do is control yourself and determine the kind of person you want to be. We can glean so much by following the example of Jesus, who loved those who lied about Him (Mark 14:59), cursed and beat Him (Matthew 26:67), rejected Him (Luke 17:25) and killed Him (John 11:53). So much cruelty, disrespect, unkindness, rejection, and negativity, yet He still loved and gave up His life for the very ones who didn't deserve it … people like you and me. Not only did He die for them, He chose to rise again! Praise the Lord! It's this powerful love that lives inside of everyone who has given their heart to Jesus. Such a love can take over our lives, give us a new heart and a renewed mind (2 Corinthians 4:16). Remember, the love of Christ gives us victory and beautiful grace to do the difficult things. So, let's decide to drop the attitudes and stop playing the victim and quit responding to the tension by being overly sensitive and dramatic or aggressive. I'm not criticizing you; I'm encouraging you because I believe in you. I know you can rise above the gossip, the rejection and the loneliness because you are a very loving person. I know you are, because if you weren't, you wouldn't have picked up this book. You wouldn't be upset or disappointed if you didn't care.

I want to confidently encourage you to not give up in your loving. I know you care about your husband and you care about the outcome of your family. It's frustrating when others can't appreciate your heart or understand your intentions, but they are not your enemy. They are your family, so love them intentionally through the love of Jesus. Extend harmony, though they may shut the door. Send the invitations, text and call to check in, cook the dinners, set up the play dates, mail the cards and attend the family gatherings. Love is an action and a choice, so don't stop. Don't get discouraged if the response doesn't reflect what you deserve. It's not about them, it's not about you and it's not even about your husband. It's about Jesus.

Ladies, we must be women our men can trust. We cannot honestly expect our husbands to have intimate, emotional and spiritual confidence in us if we are choosing to bestow unloving behavior towards the people who have raised them, supported them and cared for them throughout their lives. If we allow ourselves to write off his loved ones or declare war on his support system, it will strain your relationship with him; not theirs. On the other hand, if he is consistently observing your consideration through the conflict and recognizes your genuine attempts to resolve discord, I'm telling you he will bond closer with you in friendship as well as in intimacy. Listen, I'm cheering us all on to not grow weary in our well doing (Galatians 6:9). Keep in mind that disharmony sabotages relationships and dismantles loyalties. It's an unfortunate truth, but your love for others will preserve your marital relationship. The health and harmony of your marriage is at stake! You have the power to insert love where needed in order to soften callous hearts and infuse healing through the strength of your care and concern, which can only be fueled by the love of Christ. This doesn't mean you have to tolerate unkindness, but it does mean that God will give you the strength to extend love in all circumstances. We are in this together, friend! God is working and His plans are to use His love for your good (Romans 8:28).

Forgiveness Sets Us Free

During a very uncomfortable conversation with one of my in-laws, I was told that they had no desire to get to know me and that they did not need a relationship with me in order to have a relationship with my husband or my children. It was like someone stabbed shards of glass right into the center of my heart and the people pleaser in me was not only wounded, it was devastated. As continuous efforts were made throughout the years to reach out, to resolve issues and to show genuine love, the rejection persisted and has created great craters within the extended family structure. If I'm to be honest, the results of those hostile words and the actions that followed have been a continued spiritual battle for me.

Though I desperately want peace and restoration, this has been my "thorn in the flesh" which I am constantly seeking the Lord's healing over – not just for me, but also for the person and the other people involved. How many of us are in the same season? How many of us have endured blows by people we thought were supposed to love us? Words and actions that intentionally reject and tear down are a reflection of an insecure heart. It's this wound in them that pushes them to behave in wounding ways. But we have the anecdote! We have the love of Ch and though it can be quite offensive and confusing, we must accept the mission God has entrusted us with and therefore not allow any pain to prevent us from offering the love and forgiveness of Jesus.

Christ has called us to love without exception (Luke 6:34-35).

It's tough, but in whatever relationship that causes you offense, it's vital to stay in constant prayer to love past pain because forgiveness is where freedom lies. This is what the Lord is showing me through this trial in my life. His call to love requires obedience and not convenience. Not everyone who loves my husband is obligated to love me. Not everyone who enters our life is going to extend the chance that we deserve. It hurts, especially when it's family, but we can still love above it all because we have the power of Christ's love living within us and this love makes all things possible... including forgiveness.

If you are in a season of unforgiveness in your marriage or with your in-laws or any other relationship for that matter, I want to encourage you with this profound truth: forgiveness is a powerful force made available to us through Jesus. He calls us to Himself so that we can learn to love others as He does. He forgives freely, and so must we. Friends, forgiveness is not forgetting; it's freedom from hating what cannot be forgotten. Being told to move on is often a cop out. Getting over something that's been devastating isn't always easily done. There are consequences tied to unkindness, and the results can be permanent, which is why the Bible demands us to consider the feelings of others and respond with gentleness and compassion (Colossians 3:12). The way we treat people is so important and the way we are treated matters deeply to God. There are some words and actions and behaviors and intentions that can never be erased from our minds, but they can be erased from our hearts, in Jesus name! Understand that people are people and they will show you who they are by their actions and their words (Luke 6:45). A lack of sincerity can make forgiveness a difficult concept, but we cannot expect someone to give us what they do not possess. There may be those, even in our families, that will choose the unloving thing, but that is not who you are. It's easy to get offended, retaliate or turn our backs and cut people off out of anger, but human anger does not produce the righteousness of God (James 1:20). Forgiveness is greater.

To truly forgive is to truly be set free. Moving on without dealing with our issues isn't freedom, it's avoidance and it's immature. Being told to "get over" something that hasn't been addressed is like sweeping up dirt and then sitting in it. This is unproductive and frankly, untruthful. We have to become women who are not afraid of the truth. We have to become women who can address what is necessary and not allow the lies of unkindness to reform our identities or our security in Christ. Not every instance requires a conversation with the person, but it should result in a conversation with the Lord, allowing His Spirit to examine us, heal us and clean up anything within us that is contrary to love and forgiveness. Please remember that the only proof we have that we belong to Jesus is evident in how we love others (John 13:35). A heart that harbors unforgiveness is unpleasing to the Lord, but Christ's love prevails and empowers us to release all things with kindness.

Forgiveness, in itself, is a protection (Matthew 11: 25-26). Unforgiveness results in severed relationships with others as well as with the Lord, so I want to remind us all that since Christ so freely forgave us of our sins, the least we can do is share the same grace. Weather it's your mother in law, your sister in law, your husband, your auntie, neighbor, pastor or friend, we must forgive. Nothing should supersede your peace with God or peace in your marriage (1 Thessalonians 5:13). It honestly isn't worth it. The accusations, rejections and gossip … cast those chains down and allow the Lord's love to free you through the power of forgiveness. Scriptures declare that God's love covers us (Song of Solomon 2:4). This means that our hearts and souls are tenderly protected without fail (2 Corinthians 1:10). Since this is true for me, it is also true for you!

In all things, Christ's love covers you and keeps you (Numbers 6:24). Any battle with forgiveness doesn't make you hypocritical or ungenuine; it makes you human and it makes you honest. This is why I am so personally thankful that the Holy Spirit prays for us continuously, in our weaknesses (Romans 8:26). He is always lifting our lives before God's throne of grace because He knows we don't have the strength to do godly things on our own. The struggle sucks, but it reminds us that our inabilities and insufficiencies create deeper needs for the Lord's presence and for the power of the Holy Spirit. So, let the Lord use His love to restore you, to transform you and to equip you to grow a greater capacity to love everyone like Jesus! There is so much abounding peace and freedom for you and for your marriage, even if that means you have to forgive the same person and the same situation on a daily basis. If that's the case, do it. There is no shame in that because daily forgiveness produces daily freedom.

Boundaries that Bond Us

Your husband has the first and foremost responsibility to protect you and defend you and to uphold you (Genesis 2:4). The two of you are one flesh and one heart upheld by your covenant to one another and to God. With that being said, the Lord's command to your husband to honor and protect you does not free you from your Christian mission to love others. Our prayer must be that everyone will receive and know the love of Christ which brings freedom, clarity and harmony. God will use your love even in the middle of the mess, but our love alone cannot change anyone. Only God can do that. Until that happens, we cannot expect to see Christ from people who do not have Christ. Not everyone possesses characteristics that come from the fruit of the Spirit (Galatians 5: 22). Not everyone in our families maintain the maturity of good will. So, when discord becomes constant and concerns begin to surface, it's a mature rule of thumb that you and your husband come together and map out some boundaries to help prevent emotional and relational damage. It may be hard, but a sweet friend of mine reminded me that hard things are not wrong; they're just hard. They're uncomfortable, but not impossible.

Boundaries are important, but many of us are unaware of them until we need them. By not formulating boundaries in our lives, we're basically saying we don't deserve to be treated well. Implementing healthy boundaries proclaim that we are worthy of value and consideration. They give us guidelines for interacting with others and they are imperative to protecting what is significant to us. If there are people in our lives that behave in such a way that is less than the value God has placed over us, we need to stand up for ourselves, in loving ways by setting appropriate boundaries and executing them. This could include addressing someone's behavior, limiting the time or activities we engage with someone or simply making the choice to leave someone alone and love them from afar.

In the beginning of my marriage, I honestly thought that inserting myself was proof that I was interested in everyone. I was so eager to be a part of my new family that I did not consider how my efforts were exposing me to unhealthy personalities and environments. Looking back, I realize this was a problem I could have avoided had I instituted some boundaries. Though my intentions were good, I had made getting along about me: what can I do to change their opinion of me or persuade them to like me? My motives prevented me from setting necessary boundaries. In the end, I realized that if what I'm doing, or not doing, is for my own self-interest instead of for the Lord, then I must re-evaluate my motives. It's a confusing thing really, because we all desire to love others and have approval in some way or another, but our obedience is always better than sacrifice (1 Samuel 15:22). We cannot expect to sacrifice ourselves doing things we've not been led to do and expect flourishing results. We have to learn to wait on the Lord and seek His voice. This will equip us to practice discernment in order to decipher what is healthy and conducive for our lives, our marriages and our family. Sometimes, this involves removing ourselves for the sake of harmony and the greater good. Once we realize that something or someone is unhealthy for us, we need to use wisdom on how to navigate proper boundaries.

We are responsible to extend unity, not to force it and trust me, forcing unity never actually creates harmony. It usually produces calamity. When someone shows you who they are; believe them. Don't try to change them, because you can't. Nothing will ever be good enough to the person who doesn't see you as good enough. Your value isn't based on their opinion, anyway. It makes no sense, therefore, to continue to practice or allow the same unhealthy behaviors and expect beneficial results. We can do the loving thing within our boundaries by considering what would benefit all people involved. This does not mean that you are obligated to the demands of others, because you aren't. Your covenant is not with them; it's with your husband and it's with God, and let's be honest, they are the only people you are obligated to. So, no, you don't have to force yourself to go to the party, but you can hug the person and give them a smile when you do see them. You don't have to tolerate their manipulative tactics, but you can listen with patience. These are the gracious things. This is how we love well and how we protect the harmony within ourselves and within our marriages.

Boundaries map out healthy ways to love well. God desires to bless you and take care of all of your concerns as you and your husband work together to set appropriate boundaries for your family. Because you are his wife, you are his treasure. God has commissioned your husband to love you and protect you as Christ does for His church (Ephesians 5:25), so as you set boundaries, do so in love, not out of punishment. This will strengthen your bond and reaffirm for your husband why he chose you in the first place. Great rewards await when you love who he loves, because in doing so, you are honoring your husband's heart and showing him that you are trustworthy. On the same token, I am absolutely convinced that those who choose not to be loving towards you are unarguably disrespecting the family that your husband chose to cultivate with you. When someone decides to belittle your position as his wife, they are undermining the treasures of his heart and the vision God placed within him, because family is God's plan. Family is an inheritance and a virtue, and we are commanded by scripture to uphold it (Colossians 3:18-21). Encircling yourselves in the safety of proper boundaries will protect your relationships and establish security within your marriage and will ultimately bring the two of you closer.

Remember, Christ calls us to love everyone, every time, no matter what. Boundaries do not eliminate this opportunity; it preserves the possibility. We may find it necessary to remap our boundaries and expand them. Doing this together equips us to be considerate of each other by formulating plans that include, rather than reactions that exclude. Keep in mind that not everyone is going to agree with your boundaries; particularly those for whom the boundaries are set. It's ok if extended family are disapproving. It's ok if they don't understand. As long as your boundaries are put in place to preserve harmony, your family will benefit in the long run, even if they don't recognize it in the moment. So, give grace, draw near to

God and draw near to your husband. Ask for wisdom and discernment and then follow through with confidence. If the environment isn't healthy and the people are unwilling, I have learned that sometimes, the most loving thing to do is to eliminate the opportunity for disharmony by removing myself from the scene. Sometimes, it's best to keep a healthy distance or to remain silent out of the pursuit of peace. Let their opinions be what they'll be, but as long as our motives are aligned with the Word of God and our husbands are being honored and respected, we've done nothing wrong.

There are some people, even in our families, who are just unhealthy and unsafe, but we can use discernment and wisdom in order to establish necessary boundaries for the health of our hearts and our homes. The intentions behind our response will always say more about our character than our circumstances will, so check your motives as you explore the boundaries you choose to implement for the good of your marriage, yourself and the entirety of your family.

<u>Fear is Defeated</u>

There is something so attractive about environments of belonging and acceptance. On the other hand, arguments, gossip and the refusal to be included are such toxic experiences fueled by insecurity and jealousy and jealousy, if not dealt with, will result in competition and comparison. Ultimately, fear is birthed, which then morphs into opposition and resentment. These are real feelings which the enemy uses to populate discord and division. These are his tactics and it's all a lie.

Dr. Susan Forward, author of Toxic In-Laws: Loving Strategies for Protecting Your Marriage, tells us, "jealousy is an extension of fear … it is often not felt until after the wedding, when the new wife becomes the permanent and primary love in a man's life. This moment can be the moment everything changes in a relationship between a man's family members and his bride. This is also why and when the tension builds: the (female) family, perhaps unconsciously, blames the new wife for her feelings of replacement, and if there is any pattern or history of betrayal from other men, those feelings can emerge from past fears of rejection and lead to seeming unreasonable anger toward the new wife."[18]

Unkindness, jealousy, rejection … all are rooted in fear. It's taken me seven years to learn that. The people you're having difficulty with, they don't hate you. They are afraid that your addition is synonymous with their displacement and they are fighting to stay relevant with someone they love. They aren't the real enemy. The fear is, and it's unfortunate, but it doesn't have to be permanent.

"Perfect love casts out all fear"

- 1 John 4:18 (ESV)

---

[18] Forward, S. (2010, September 07). Toxic In-Laws - Loving Strategies for Protecting Your Marriage - Read book online. Retrieved August 14, 2020, from https://r24spre.24symbols.net/book/english/susan-forward/toxic-in-laws---loving-strategies-for-protecting-your-marriage?id=1308978

God is love. Perfect love; the closer we draw to Him, the closer He will draw nearer to us (James 4:8). Salvation results in a total God take over and where there is God, fear must flee (2 Timothy 1:7). What does this have to do with loving who our husband loves? It has everything to do with it! If God is perfect love and perfect love casts out fear, then our salvation in Christ makes it possible for us to be courageous in environments of rejection and intimidation. There is no fear when God is near! Some of you have beautiful friendships within your extended family. Some of you have cordial relationships with your husband's support system, and that's a blessing. But no one can go through life without conflict with someone at some point in time. That's just life. Conflict is coming and with it comes fear and anxiety, but the presence of God will sustain you through it all.

It's hard to reach out and love and forgive when we are fearful. It's difficult to walk in confidence when we are afraid. But a scripture that has been so important to me reminds me that the Lord is on my side, so I don't need to fear, and that people do not have power over me (Psalm 118: 6). I've not been perfect in remembering and meditating on this all the time, but I am learning to trust the Lord when I'm afraid and offer it up to Him in exchange for His presence which always pushes back my anxieties and uncertainties.

The occurrence of conflict can be the result of someone's fear. Whoever they are, they are afraid of losing someone they love; they are afraid that you have replaced their significance. You all have a very dynamic interest in common: your husband! He is the object of affection and it's his allegiance that's being vied for, but loving can soothe the fear. Loving can abolish the assumptions. The lack of love on your part could confirm the very fear that God's perfect love desires to cast out. It's as simple as that. Fear causes us to retreat or attack; neither is productive and neither allows us to share the perfect love of God with those who need to see it.

Never forget that our families are our calling and a commission Christ has entrusted us with in order to run on mission in serving others rather than ourselves. Love and kindness is a fruit of the Spirit (Galatians 5:22). Unconditional love and kindness can only be manifested through a relationship with Jesus and the infilling of His Holy Spirit because such things are eternal, not momentary. Flesh is born of flesh, but the Spirit gives birth into eternal things (John 3:6). Once we recognize the distinction of loving by the power of the Holy Spirit, we will be much better equipped to run our race with endurance when it comes to loving difficult people. It will never be easy, though. You will have to give up something when you choose this path. You will have to give up your right to be heard sometimes. You will have to give up your pride, your control, your way and your resentment. But the sacrificing of these things is how God teaches us and transforms us into the beautiful image of His Son. You have been called to do this; therefore, you are equipped and capable!

No one should be given the permission to come between you and your man or you and your God. I know the stirring thoughts that like to scream in our minds. I know the struggle and the fear and the confusion, but I also know that you are more than a conqueror in every situation (Romans 8:37)! No weapon will prosper against you or against your marriage unless you allow it to. So, don't allow it to. Don't give fear space in your heart or in your mind. It's uninvited and it's not in control. The love of Christ is in control and we must learn to place all negative thoughts at His feet by calling out the lies, refusing to rehearse them in our minds and reminding ourselves who we are in Christ: purposed (Ephesians 1:4), blessed (Psalm 146: 5) and a beautiful light in the world (Matthew 5:14). This is the identity that is available to us all through a relationship with Jesus and it's this very identity that will keep your marriage set apart and seated in Heavenly places – above the drama, above the lies and above any fear that desires to distract you from loving well.

My prayer for all of us is to stay focused on what truly matters. Your marriage is more sacred than any other relationship. It's easy to get distracted by the confusion of conflict around you, but through Jesus, we can love past our fears. We can elevate our marriages above disharmony through the love and kindness that we show and share. We can include the people our husband loves, reach out to them and pray for them. We can extend a helping hand to them, though they may slap it away. Remember, it's not them doing it. Not really. It's their fear and fear is their bondage. But you, my darling, you live in freedom. Your heart is filled to the brim with the love of Christ and therefore fear has no place and no hold over you. You have the power to love, in spite of everything. You can do it! You are doing it. So. keep doing it.

Uniting the Divided

Harmony is in the heart of God (Psalms 133:2) and therefore it should be our heart's desire, as well. Because our mission is to point to God in everything we say and do, we know that we can't protect our hearts or fight against such deceptions with human efforts. We have to use spiritual weapons that only come from the Holy Spirit (Ephesians 6:10-18). Rejection, disharmony, unkindness and lack of peace does not come from the Lord. These are spiritual toxins sponsored by the enemy and it's his desire to confuse you into thinking the problem is the person that you see, rather than the invisible sin and internal struggle that you cannot see (Ephesians 6:12).

If we are handling conflict based on our fleshly feelings, we will never operate with spiritual clarity, grace or understanding. This will prevent us from seeing the unique opportunities that the Lord has entrusted us with to show his love to people who are hurting and broken (Proverbs 3:5-6). Listen, broken people do broken things. Don't let broken people break you. Don't let the brokenness of the enemy's lies cause you to break away from your faith, your hope or your trust in God and the good work He has promised to produce in you and in your marriage (Philippians 1:6).

Even as I am typing this to you, I'm wiping tears from my left cheek. The pain of feeling mistreated is bitter and if I am honest, there have been times where I chose to push people away in the name of self-preservation; but, for me, this resulted in more hurt and more disharmony. I must be quite honest and admit to you all that I haven't always made Christ-centered decisions when it comes to responding to disharmony. I haven't always reminded myself that I have the victory in Jesus and that He is my strength and my light. Everything I am writing to you, I am living it, too. I am making mistakes and internally struggling with how to love when it' s difficult and how to forgive when it seems impossible. I'm trying and praying for God's grace to heal and transform me. I know you're praying the same things. I know you desire to love fully and completely, in redemptive forgiveness and merciful grace. It's the desire of our hearts because we love our husbands and we love our Lord. My prayer for us all is to continue to run on mission and to love in whatever manner Christ makes available in our lives. We can do this, ladies! We can be the light and we can pray for unity as we raise our families and love like Jesus.

I'm not sure if anyone is ever truly to blame. It's like that riddle, "Who came first? The chicken or the egg?" Who started it first? Who's to blame? Who knows? But what I do know is though you may feel justified in feeling offended, your feelings will never justify any decision to behave in unloving ways. It doesn't matter who started it. It doesn't matter if they were wrong or condescending or excluding or rude. Loving people love people and if you love your husband, it is imperative that you love who he loves in order to build flourishing unity together, within your families and with God.

"Beloved, let us love one another, for love is from God, and whoever loves has been born of God and knows God. Anyone who does not love does not know God, because God is love. Beloved, if God so loved us, we also ought to love one another. No one has ever seen God; but if we love one another, God lives in us and his love is made complete in us."

-1 John 4: 7-12 (NIV)

The love of Christ compels us to be loving to everyone, even the most difficult of people. If you can't love people, you can't love God and you must love God in order to have a God-centered marriage. When it is all said and done, I desire to be a woman who is consumed with pleasing Jesus and I want to love people with the same passion in which He loves me! I know that's what you want, too! I'm in no way perfect at all, but I am learning to reach out with grace. No one can understand the love we have is genuine if they aren't given the opportunity to see it in action. We can't expect to be lights if we insist on being hidden. Listen, you are just as much an in-law to them as they are to you. You are each other's family now. It's time to seek the Lord on how to unite what may have been divided because division is in opposition of God's abundant life for you.

Love who your husband loves, even though they may not love you. Be kind. Be gracious. Within your boundaries, invite opportunities to include them and always, always pray for them. You can make efforts to unite the divided relationships simply by reaching out and remaining available to them because we serve a God of redemption who delights in harmony.

"Live in harmony with one another"
– Romans 12:16 (ESV)

A woman who desires to love well desires the spiritual maturity required to extend grace and to find a place for everyone. This doesn't mean that you owe anyone a close seat, but what this does mean is that you can choose to extend an invited place at the table, should they desire to sit and participate.

As we love who our husbands love, we are actually doing so as unto the Lord. He will guide you and give you grace if you ask Him (Luke 12:31). Realize, going forward, that not everyone is going to receive your welcome and not everyone is going to want what you want. Not everyone is going to choose to sit and enjoy the love you have to offer, but the love of Christ in you will position your heart to extend that invitation of inclusion in however He chooses to lead you, regardless of the outcome. You can be confident in your approach to share the love of Christ with those who have hurt you and you can rest assured that it will bring about more blessings for your life and for your marriage. We cannot control others, but we can control our willingness to extend love and grace and the goodness of God to anyone the Lord has seen fit to place in our lives. The acceptance of our invitation is entirely up to them.

Reflection

Think of anyone in your husband's life who has been particularly challenging to get along with. Say a prayer over this person and ask God to give you wisdom on how to love them and show them grace.

<u>Scriptures for Your Soul</u>

"Be kind to one another, tenderhearted, forgiving one another, as God in Christ forgave you."

- Ephesians 4:32

CHAPTER 7

SWEET MYSTERIES

Ok, ok, here we go! The chapter we've all been waiting for! The juicy stuff! The orgasmic tell-all's! Ha! Why are we so intrigued when it comes to discussing sex? Is it because religion makes it seem shameful, but society makes it so enticing? What's the truth in it all? Is sex good or bad? Is good sex good or bad? Should godly women be interested in their sexuality? Does sex get better throughout the entirety of our marriage or is it something that only lasts until the kids come? My answer to all of this is yes and no. Much of it depends on the couple, their situation, their health, their desire and their relationship with one another and their relationship with God; yes, God.

I am here to declare to us all, with sheets wrinkled and pillows tossed around, that sex was crafted and created by our Heavenly Father who loves and adores us and only offers us good things. Sex is a good thing because it's God's incredible gift to us for our marriage. In our unions, we should all be open to explore the sensuality of sex in creative and freeing ways! It's ours to enjoy with pleasure and without measure within our marriages. There are a lot of lies our culture feeds us about our sexuality and many of us,even in our marriages, are unsure about the proper use of sex and therefore struggle to experience the fullness of our sexuality. But I believe that sex is delicious and lovely and blessed! It's just as spiritual as it is physical and I'm looking forward to sharing my perspective with you about such a taboo topic. I must be upfront, however, and warn you that there may be some points that I present that you may not agree with or may make you feel uncomfortable. Many of us come from various backgrounds and upbringings and have made choices in our lives that may not align with one another when it comes to this very personal topic, but I dare you to read everything in this chapter because we're going somewhere good! Just stay with me because we will be uncovering some exciting terrain, and I don't want you to miss out on where we're headed!

<u>What You Need to Know</u>

There is so much confusion around sex and we know that God is not the author of confusion (1 Corinthians 14:33). I want to encourage you to trust that God wants to bless your marital sex life and flourish it for your good and His glory! A woman's body was crafted to desire her man and we already know that men were designed with cravings to explore the body of a woman. Frankly speaking, we were made with an innate curiosity and longing to be connected and to be fulfilled, sexually. In Genesis, God tells Eve that she will always desire her husband (Genesis 3:16). This was the first indication ever made concerning how sex seals us to the person we've taken into our bodies. And though the world has altered the meaning of sex and has re-defined the use of it, the fact of the matter is that God created our bodies to be cherished and connected, not to be used for control, power or self-fulfillment.

Obviously, because the enemy in this world hates all things divine, it's no shock that he would deploy plans to alter, manipulate and pervert our lovely sexuality. But we can take back our freedom by unapologetically declaring that as married women, we do desire to be sexually intimate with our husbands and there's nothing inappropriate about that! Engaging in marital sex is a delight for our bodies and a form of obedience to God (Genesis 1:28). In addition, the benefits of sex can extend beyond the bedroom. Studies verify that love making improves our health, boosts immunity and creates an intimate psychological connection between the two individuals [19]. It creates confidence, allows us to express what sometimes our words simply cannot and contributes to a nurturing environment, which children will thrive in. Putting it plainly, there are multifaceted purposes in it all. God designed our love making to be very, very physical, but it's also very, very spiritual. It's where the knitting of souls takes place, as the body and spirit of each person fuse together during the experience; literally, the two becoming one. The

---

[19] Charnetski, Carl J., and Francis X. Brennan. "Sexual Frequency and Salivary Immunoglobulin." Psychological Reports, vol. 94, no. 3, June 2004, pp. 839–844

Bible mentions this phenomenon four times (Genesis 2:24; Matthew 19:5; Mark 10:8; Ephesians 5:3); pointing to its importance, not only for creating life, but for living life. I believe there is something to this rapidity and something to miss out should one not be considerate of the spiritual impacts involved in the physical experience of sexual exchange. This should be exciting and freeing, yet, because of previous misuse, many of us struggle with the sensual oneness that occurs by the fusing together of hearts and genitalia. Some of us hesitate from our freedom because we confuse sex with sin. So, let's just make it clear here in this safe space: God created sex for marriage, therefore, having sex with your husband is not sinful because God does not create sin (1 John 1:15). Everything He has created is good (1 Timothy 4:4), thus sex experienced within His design of marriage is a good thing to do.

God approves of your marital sex! Yes, you read that correctly (Genesis 1:28). God wants you to enjoy the depths of your sexuality with your husband and He wants you to enjoy the pleasures of sensual fulfillment and exchange within your marriage. This is what you need to know! It's why He built our bodies with sexual organs specifically to stimulate pleasure. It's His strategic plan for His creation, but when creation restructures what has been divinely fashioned, it is morally wrong to then expect divine results. When we choose to engage in our sexuality outside of the covenant of marriage, which it was designed for, it's blasphemous to expect the blessings of God to abound in the action. Simply put, choosing our desires over God's instructions is wrong. We can't reject His ways and then request His approval. There is order to His creation and the order for sex is marriage.

Now those of you who are already married may assume that this does not apply to you; but I warn you that it does. The Bible says that even if we think about sexual acts with someone we are not married to, it's immoral (Matthew 5:28). And many of us, either aware or unaware, might be partaking in sexual immorality within our marriages. How so? Well, it's in the everyday decisions we compromise to make for the sake of self-pleasure or social acceptance. Stay with me now, because it's an area we all need to search our hearts and renew our minds about.

Even as married women, we need to know that we must always guard our hearts and our minds from being tainted by the world's deception and false depiction of love and sex in our marriages. Watching movies with elicit scenes, looking at magazines that wet our sexual appetite, reading books that entice us to sexually fantasize over men who do not exist, even conversations with friends that do not edify our marriages…these things expose us to other people who we are not married to and therefore is outside of God's design for marriage. I know it sounds extreme, but anything done outside of God's design and order is disobedience and disobedience is sin. But we are conflicted, aren't we, because our world tells us that our rights and preferences are more valuable than God's Word. Our society promotes sexual immorality so openly and makes it so easily available, we've become immune to it and therefore susceptible to falling entrapped by it. It's so subtle, we forget to examine it. We just click, flip, and scroll away, without a thought as to whether or not what we are taking in is pleasing to Christ.

There are spiritual ramifications to everything we do in the flesh. "When we connect so intimately outside of a marriage relationship … our personal identity (and) design becomes fractured." [20] This is a quote from my sweet friend in the UK, Bobbi Kumari, who has written a book called *Sacred Sexuality*, and in it, she shares how a relationship with the Lord re-shaped her mindset on God's freedom for a healthy and thriving sex life. Sex is sacred. A thriving sex life in your marriage is made up of more than one another's genitalia. Our sexual drive is a beautiful thing that God saw fit to bless us with, so we have to protect the purity of it. We need to embrace that we are sexual beings and we have to be responsible with our sexuality – guarding our eyes from the lust of this world, keeping our hearts from comparisons with other people's marriages and aligning our lives with the principles of godly loving and living as shown to us in scripture.

The Bible tells us that even if our thoughts are impure, we have sinned (Matthew 5:27-28). Talking about fantasies involves thinking about them. Watching sex on TV – you're thinking about it. Listening along to songs that promote sexual impurity – your brain is pondering it. Reading racy novels where character's sexual exploits are being described in detail … well, we know how that

---

[20] Kumari, B. *Sacred Sexuality: Rewire Your Desire Towards True Intimacy.* Living in Light, 2019.

plays out in our minds. It might seem like harmless little indulgences, but they plant weeds in our hearts and in our marriages. Over time, they sprout into spiritual desensitization which aim to sabotage our intimacy and our exclusivity.

What you need to know is that anything done outside of God's instructions is not His best for you, therefore, it will never render His ample blessings over you. A woman who desires to love well understands that sex with her husband is holy; sex without her husband is not. In marriage, your sexual acts, your sexual thoughts, your sexual imaginations and participation is for your husband. Only. Some of us, even married women, have not taken this command seriously. Either out of rebellion or out of ignorance, we've been guilty of toying with sexual immorality in some form or fashion. Some of us entered into sexual encounters before our marriages, some have gone to the strip clubs or have clicked on those website links or even slightly fondled with the pleasure of private messages we've received on social media. We've looked at our co-worker a bit too long, we've flirted with scenes on TV and we've entertained the inappropriate compliment we received in passing. Include your own example where it applies. None of us are immune to enticement and I understand those temptations are real. The Bible says that Jesus understands them, too (Hebrews 4:15), but you have the power of Christ to say no to things that will not serve your mission to love your husband well. We cannot expect to love our men until we learn to love God and loving God is never accomplished when we choose our flesh in disobedience; I don't care what society tells you.

Any pursuit or acceptance of intimacy and sexual experience outside of God's design leaves us with a fraction of the wondrous gift He desires to offer us. We've all fallen short. Sometimes, even in marriage, we may randomly endure consequences of past faces and places that flash in our memory against our will. These are the shames that sin never prepares us for, but I want you to know that's not what sex, God's way, was designed to produce in your life. God's rewards for you are always freeing, pure, holy, virtuous, lovely, righteous and blessed! These are the eternal rewards for living and loving in obedience to God's design; no regrets attached! God only creates good things which, when used obediently, produces better things. Marriage isn't all about sex, of course, but sex was created for marriage, only, and when used according to its purpose, it permeates a form of worship and true joy.

I have no interest in highlight anyone's mistakes, but to point us to the holy love of God, which He desires to bestow upon your life and into your marriage. No one is perfect. No one is holy or righteous and therefore no one has a place to condemn you for anything done in your past (Romans 3:11-12). None of us, not even a virgin, is exempt from the temptation of sexual sin. Marriage doesn't eliminate this, and singleness isn't unique to temptation, but we can all rest in the freedom of obedience at any time and trust the Lord to renew our minds and create clean hearts within us as we move forward in loving well. We need to know this and hold tight to this because it's this truth that should be exploding in our marital sex lives! I know it's a radical notion in our society, but I cannot, in good conscious, discuss sex without addressing this very sincere truth. There is nothing more freeing than being at one with your husband and being at one with your God! The application of godliness in our sexuality can make all the difference in our marriage and in our sex lives. It's yours for the taking and for the love making!

God, Sex and You

Last year, I was asked to speak to a group of lovely ladies from all over North Carolina who gathered to mingle, pray and grow deeper in their understanding of love and relationship with Christ. When talking about forgiveness, faith, how to find your purpose and ways to grow spiritually … oh, they had no problem talking and chatting and sharing. But when it came to the topic assigned to me, which was marriage and sex, the room went dead silent. Suddenly, these confident, accomplished women turned into squeamish little girls, all giggling and afraid to speak. Finally, I was asked this question by a brave college student who sat in the middle row:

"What are the rules for sex within a Christian marriage?"

Boom! The bomb dropped. Every lady leaned in closer with anticipation so thick and savory, you could have eaten it. These professional, devout women were aching for the reply. Women had stopped taking notes. Some were smirking and others looked completely shocked and restless for the answer. Butterflies filled my heart as I began to speak. I smiled at all of them and then gave my response.

"No extra people".

Seas of gasps and giggles filled the room and I knew we had finally crossed over into the conversation of no return. It was the most incredible speaking engagement I've ever participated in! Awkward questions turned into confident conversations as women of all ages and all seasons began to share and explore God's Word on sex and how it applies and progresses our marital experiences.

Though the Bible doesn't disclose every specific sexual act a couple can experience in their marriage, it does propose a loving context and passionate clues in books such as Song of Solomon and other areas throughout scripture. Sex is celebrated in the Bible; therefore, it should be celebrated in our bedrooms! In marriage, God gives us the green light to go. And go. And go! So, the concern shouldn't be in how to have sex, but rather in becoming better love makers, which always requires selfless giving and intentional receiving.

There is reckless celebration to be explored within our marriages and we've each been given the invitation of holiness in our union and freedom in our sexuality to love our husbands well while being pleasing to the Lord. Sex, through God's design, is so very holy and thrilling and life-giving, as well as life-making! My prayer is that we receive this, unapologetically, and practice it often!

"The husband should fulfill his wife's sexual needs, and the wife should fulfill her husband's needs. The wife gives authority over her body to her husband, and the husband gives authority over his body to his wife."
— 1 Corinthians 7: 3-4 (ESV)

This is an instruction that we should be obeying! We have divine permission and commission to enjoy our sexuality within the union and relationship of our marriages. This is God's design and He is telling us to give ourselves over to one another to meet the sexual needs, drives and desires that He placed within us to enjoy. Too many women have a conflicting depiction of sex simply because the world misuses it. But not all sex is shameful or raunchy or immoral. Your marriage makes your sex pure and pleasing and beautiful and acceptable. Your marriage makes your sex moral. You don't have to feel awkward or question whether or not something is allowed or appropriate or holy in your marriage. If it's between you and your husband and you both are enjoying one another, God gives us permission to carry on!

Boring marital sex, or worse, boring Christians having boring marital sex is such an inaccurate and absurd stereotype. It's my personal belief that as Christians, we should be having the best sex of all, because we have the blessings of God for our marriage while we are living and loving as unto the Lord (2 Corinthians 9:8). What we do in our marriage, where we do it, how and when we do it is up to us, as long as it maintains the marital guidelines God has given us as scripture has laid out (Matthew 19:4-6). God's instruction on loving our spouse in physical and spiritual totality should have us all excited and confident! The Lord isn't opposed or disgusted by your need to be desired or to be physically fulfilled. There are plenty of scriptures that encourage sexual expression and invitation between husbands and wives: to enjoy one another's bodies and to enjoy the fulfilments of our sexual drive, over and over again.

"Blow on my garden, that its spices may flow out.
Let my beloved come into his garden and taste his precious fruits."
-Song of Songs 4:16 (NLT)

Go ahead and read that again. I won't tell!

A common debate regarding this scripture speculates if it's talking about intercourse or oral sex. To be completely honest, I don't know, and I don't care, because I applaud both! Our sexuality is a God-given gift meant for marriage and it should be celebrated, freely, within our marriages. We have so much freedom to explore the gift of one another's love, with confidence and without shame because guilt is only present in the absence of obedience. But our Creator gave us sex as a gift in the obedience of our marriages. So, we can celebrate our marital sexuality as unto the Lord by loving with respect and devotion as declared in Romans 12:10. This is holy and blessed by God, who crafted our bodies in particular ways to enjoy pleasure with one another in the sacredness of marriage.

Going Deeper

A clear message can be noted in scripture: devotion must be present in our exploration. It's what elevates our motives from being self-focused and into selflessly loving. Devoted love doesn't engage in sexual actions that are demeaning, hurtful, embarrassing or forceful; this includes harmful objects. That is not the love of God. In addition, God-centered love, according to scripture, doesn't include pornography because that's not following Christ's instructions and warnings against lust (1 Thessalonians 4: 3-5). The holiness and purity of sex is marked by monogamous celebration and an exclusion of outside individuals, in every way, shape or form. Since the covenant is with one another, then the sex must be exclusively reserved for the individuals who are bound by that covenant.

Even in a good marriage with good sex, we know that the thrill of passion is short lived. No sex will save a floundering marriage. No amount of foreplay, roleplay, or orgasms can duplicate a union that's been built God's way. It's not supposed to, because everything done in the flesh fades away (1 Peter 1:4). God desires more for your marriage than a fleeting experience a few times a week. You may not agree, and that's your choice, but I believe God's word, totally and completely (Sola Scriptura), and I believe that He wants our lives filled with eternal goodness, not just passive pleasures that only skim at the surface of our physical indulgences. He wants us to dive deep into the experience of a lush and fulfilling marriage and the spiritual growth that marriage provides. As we grow in Him, we begin to grow with one another in ways that our anatomy can never replicate. You see, marital sex is designed to point us to the deeper divinity of God and His selfless, unconditional, spiritual and unifying love for us, through Jesus. This isn't always easy or comfortable and the lessons our lives lead us into, which are there to shape us, can become a hindrance to us if we have not secured our marriages into the unconditional love of God. Pleasure is conditional. Feelings, passion, romance ... these things are conditional and will never lead us into deeper spiritual maturity, growth or relationship with our husbands or with the Lord.

We know that worship takes place in our souls and thus occurs whenever God's creation does what it was created to do within the precepts of God's ordinances (Psalm 66:4). So, sex is truly a form of worship and worship is a deep spiritual experience manifested through physical expressions. When it comes to sex, it is my Christian belief that genitalia are only a surfaced aspect. There are deeper things still. Culture publishes and pushes on us that breasts and vaginas, hands, mouths and penises play the essential role in intercourse and that when used correctly, these physical exchanges will prove that love is unfolding or determine compatibility or romance. Hands, shoulders, knees and toes ... if it's just about the body and the feelings, we've fractured the truth of what sex is and should be. We have to go deeper than that (pun intended)!

"Too many of us have bought into the idea that sex is primarily a physical thing … but if we see sex only in the physical realm, we've degraded the experience." [21] This quote was extracted from *The Good Girls Guide to Great Sex*. It opposes the popular notion that sex is about self-discovery: what we like, what we feel, what we can do, how we can do it. If that's all that our sexuality is about – that personal preference and pleasure is what generates good sex – we don't really need a man for that, and we don't need marriage, either. But this is the direction our society has chosen and sadly, many couples who claim Christ aren't walking in obedience when it comes to their sexuality.

Marriage is about mission, not pleasure, yet there are pleasures released as we obediently run on mission to please the Lord in all that we do, including our sex lives. God desires us to grow: as individuals, as wives, as mothers and as His ambassadors for the Gospel. This is exactly why God forbids pre-marital sex, because a lack of covenant leaves no invitation for spiritual growth. Covenant will cultivate your conflicts into maturity and into mission. Sex, therefore, is the result of our unions, not the reason. On the surface, it may seem as if the lines of love and sex are blurred; but as we dive deeper in God's design for marriage, we soon uncover that love

---

[21] Gregoire, Sheila Wray. *The Good Girl's Guide to Great Sex:* (And You Thought Bad Girls Have All the Fun), Zondervan, 2012.

produces sex; not the other way around. God's love is the orchestrator of your marriage. Let Him lead you into the deep places that only His love can reveal.

Body, Spirit, Soul

Sitting in the car one afternoon, I decided to tune into the latest podcast I had guested on. It was a Biblical conversation on our sexual drives in light of God's design. Once it ended, the next episode (or so I thought) began to play. It didn't take long for me to realize that I was no longer listening to a Christian based show on love and marriage. The hosts were discussing the empowerment of teaching young girls how to masturbate and self-stimulate with sex toys and imaginative fantasies. Stunned and disgusted, I began fumbling with my phone to turn it off. I was horrified that such a misuse of God's gift was being encouraged to the masses of young and impressionable women.

Listen ladies, I know it's widely accepted, but if we buy into the lie that the point of sex is to discover and fulfill our own physical interests first before we are able or capable of satisfying our husbands, what's the point in worrying about our souls? So many of us have fallen under the weight of this cheap propaganda and we have soul-ties and deep scars from broken relationships to prove it. This was never the Lord's intentions for your body, your spirit or your soul. Brokenness was never a part of His original design for your heart. Christ came to give us a full life in every extent of our existence and this includes our souls; not just our bodies.

When we neglect to take care of our spirits and our souls in our sexual involvement and experiences, we are ignoring a vital portion of ourselves, and therefore, it cannot truly be self-discovery that we are exploring if our souls are being overlooked. Your soul is just as much a part of you as your body is and it's involved in sex just as much as your vagina is and therefore, if ignored, the spiritual aspect of one's sexual engagements will have adverse effects in one's life. This is because sex wasn't designed for carnal exploration. It's so much more than that. You're not a rabbit or a dog or any other animal that goes around mindlessly humping out of instinct; neither are you an empty instrument in need of being filled with fragments of leftovers from compromise. You have been called out, commissioned and set apart.

Keep in mind that our God is not one-dimensional. He is majestic in all His ways. There is deep purpose in sex within our marriages. Consider that flowers are beautiful and medicinal. The ocean produces oxygen and crops, just as the land does. Your sex is for your body as well as for your spirit. The divine design for sex was never to serve the skin and bones. Its purpose penetrates beneath the surface of our physical composition and into a spiritual application of scripture and covenant. With this being so, we can take pleasure in our marriage through the exploration of sex with our husbands, in purity and in holiness, as long as we are in line with scripture and devotion to one another, under the sheets or wherever else it may occur. This doesn't offend the Lord, it pleases Him, because our obedience is edifying and an edified marriage points to the Gospel.

Remember, you are a soul that lives inside a body and that soul was created to glorify your Father in Heaven (Luke 1:46). You are also a spirit, which is more real than your body, because your body will one day decompose; but your spirit will live forever (Ecclesiastes 12:7). Underneath it all, you are an immortal and eternal being. What takes place in your body will produce results in other areas of your existence. Your soul is precious, and it is your essence. It's deep down and it's effected by everything you do. It's invisible, but it's not impenetrable! There is no doubt in my mind that the deep, sensual, blissful and pleasurable sex that our souls truly crave can only take place within the covenant of marriage because marriage, like sex, is spiritual.

Please understand that your marriage is symbolic of God's holy love and eternal unity with His people. A woman who desires to love well understands that the sex which occurs within her marriage has been blessed to penetrate deeper than mere physical participation. It's in this aspect of our unions where we tangibly exemplify oneness and sacred grace. This is God's reward of blessing our obedience and molding us, through marriage, to be ambassadors of His unfailing love. This is what happens in the deep places of God: commitment, covenant and relationship, where two souls join in the mutual mission of loving one another, with the unconditional love of Christ.

An Exclusive Invitation

One of the highlights of my bridal showers was opening pretty boxes wrapped in ribbon, which contained sexy little lingerie inside! Screams and squeals from my friends filled the room as I threw tissue paper onto the floor and extracted outfits meant for married women only. But, in today's society, undergarments aren't kept secret anymore. Lace and garters aren't considered marriage material anymore. The modern view has declared that the sacred things, like sensually luring our husbands, should no longer be an exclusive invitation, but rather a public show of feminism.

Ladies, the purpose of our sexual expression was never meant for public display. As Christ followers, we understand that our bodies are not our own (1 Corinthians 6:19). Wearing outfits that expose our "lovely lady lumps" does not fall in line with honoring our bodies as the temple of God and I strongly believe that the present generation of Christian sisters and brothers need to consider the sanctity of sexuality for the purpose of pleasing Jesus, protecting our witness and pleasuring our marriages with dignity and exclusivity.

Listen, your sex is a beautiful thing, but it wasn't designed to be flaunted as an open demonstration. Sex is just as much sacred as it is sensual. So, I wonder, where are we getting our instructions from? Is it from the billion-dollar entertainment industry or from the Bible? Either we follow the carnality of the flesh which leads to destruction or we follow Christ, which leads us to life and blessings (Matthew 7:13-14).

In the book of 1 Corinthians, Paul tells us that every personal choice is permissible, but not all choices are beneficial.

"I have the right to do anything," you say--but not everything is beneficial. "I have the right to do anything"--but not everything is constructive."
— 1 Corinthians 10:23

You have the right to show what you want to show and pose how you want to pose, but in light of eternity and, in regards to your marriage, and your representation of Christ, are skin-revealing clothing or spandex mini dresses spiritually constructive? I dare you to answer that question because dressing our bodies takes intentionality. Are we using our intentionality to consider why we do what we do or dress how we dress? Are our outfits for the glory of God or for the glory of our sexuality?

All women want to dress well and there is nothing wrong with that at all, but how are we dressing? That's the question. Trends change, culture changes, but God's Word remains the same and His Bible teaches that we, as His name bearers, should be holy, pure and modest (1 Peter 3:4). People need to see Jesus when they look at our lives, wardrobes, and self-expressions. They need to see that our freedoms in Christ exemplify Christ, not the world. It's unfortunate, but I've encountered other people's lingerie while I shop in the grocery store just as easily as when I scroll through social media. It saddens me to see that the sweetness of seduction has been replaced with irreverent styles that leave nothing for the imagination. No longer is lingerie purchased for the bedroom – people are wearing it out to dinner! We're cheering women on who dress themselves in immodesty, as if it is courageous to do so. Our peers – and even some of us – are eagerly sharing with the world what should be kept hidden, but there is spiritual danger in doing this.

In the book of Revelation, Jesus addresses a community that tolerates what He called a "Jezebel Spirit". Jesus makes no apologies in addressing this church directly and abhorring their practice of immodesty.

"I have this against you, that you tolerate that woman Jezebel."
– Revelation 2:20 (ESV)

In early history, B.C., Jezebel was a corrupt queen who seduced her way into power. The connotation of the name Jezebel is "virtuous woman", but her nature was in complete defiance of the meaning. She was a gruesome woman, in character, but ravishing and alluring in her features. You can read her story in 1 Kings in the Bible, but basically, she was a beautiful woman who paraded her sexuality as a means to control her husband and get what she wanted from other powerful men. She murdered the prophets, tormented God's people and died a most disgusting death – being pushed out a window and eaten alive by dogs. Not a very beautiful picture, is it?

What I find interesting is that Jesus addresses her spirit among the churches in Revelation. Centuries later, her vile essence was still found rampant, not only in the world, but also in the church. Racing like a nymph in naked obstinance, her spirit is still loose today and beacons power and attention through sexual means; not because she's interested in those who give her attention, but because she lusts after their attraction. Notice in the scripture that the Lord doesn't say that He is offended by Jezebel. Nope, He's offended by those who tolerate her. He's offended by those who entertain her and allow themselves to be influenced and lured away by her.

Ladies, we need to recognize the foul influence that the spirit of Jezebel can have on us and even within our marriages. The Lord didn't like her spirit in Revelation, and He doesn't like it now. He scolded His church for engaging her appeal while claiming to have His holiness because sexual immorality isn't independent to singleness. If we are not grounded in scripture, following trends and culture could place us in spiritual danger of tolerating worldly impurity in our marital lives.

It may seem ill placed to include this portion in a marital book, but I am concerned for our generation when it comes to providing an open invitation into the realm of our sexuality. Our bodies are for our husbands and for the Lord, only. They're not even for ourselves (1 Corinthians 6: 20). The finesse of marital seduction is sweet between the two of you, only, as you enjoy one another and explore each other, God's way. Publicly showing more than is necessary is not glorifying to God, neither is it the gentle spirit that scripture says is beautiful in the eyes of the Lord (1 Peter 3: 3-4). I dare say we aren't even honoring our husbands any longer either, if we expose private areas that attract onlookers. It's unholy, ungodly and unloving. It's grotesque to Jesus and should be grotesque to us.

Tolerating Jezebel doesn't mean you're having sex with other people; it means you're exposing your sex to other people. See the difference? As a former fashion model, I must admit to you all that I've had to rewire some of my thinking over the years and allow the Lord to renew my mind when it comes to how I should dress myself. The modeling world had an influence on me in many ways, but I am discovering that God's glory is what I desire most. His presence is radiant and that's the only attention we should be longing for. Everything else is fleshly and we know that the flesh leads to death (James 1:15). Carnal attention from this world could never compare to the riches God has adorned you with in Christ Jesus, nor the exclusive seduction He has made available to you within your marriage. Your breasts and hips and thighs weren't fashioned for public observation. You don't have to succumb to immodest displays of yourself in order to validate your beauty or your worth. You are not your curves, anyway. Christ has called you out from the crowd, has placed His crown on your head and calls you daughter (2 Corinthians 6:18). There is a difference between being confident with our bodies and being wise enough to know what should be kept a sweet mystery for our husbands and their exclusive delight.

Even in marriage, if we are seeking sexual approval or attention from people other than our husbands, how can we expect to cultivate exclusivity in our monogamy? If we are following emotionless examples of worldly women, draping ourselves with trends that invite lust from outsiders or filling our heads with raunchy images that have more to do with individualism than selfless loving, how can we expect to cultivate holy and exclusive love in our marriages? A woman who desires to love well chooses to dress herself in ways that complement her beauty, rather than exposing her sexuality. There should be a sweetness in our sexuality within our marriages as we choose to love each other, God's way. But outside of that realm, exposing our sexuality will lead us to tread into treacherous spiritual territories.

Ladies, the problem is not in our closets and it's not in the technology of social media, either. The problem is what's in our hearts – our motives behind how we are presenting ourselves and the intentions that fuel our reasonings. Our choices convey a message, so we must be considerate of the messages we are expressing to the world and save our seductions for our husbands because our bodies are for our them and their bodies are for us (1 Corinthians 7:3-4). Each curve is a gift to satisfy his needs and desires, just as his anatomy is a gift meant only for us to enjoy. Inciting onlookers to admire our sexuality, either in the way we dress, the way we pose for pictures or the conversations we have, is embarking on Jezebel's spirit, which is rebellious, dishonoring and impure. Anything of great worth should be limited to the one it is meant for. It's in the exclusivity that forges the opulence.

"I will not look with approval on anything that is vile. I hate what faithless people do; I will have no part in it."
-Psalm 101:3 (NIV)

Ladies, we need to live lives that the Lord desires to look

upon. Displaying our sexuality to anyone other than our husband crosses some very serious lines that offend the Lord and tarnish our witness. I dare say that many provocative outfits aren't worn by women who truly feel beautiful but, rather, worn by those who desire the rush associated with being told they are beautiful. This is a Jezebel spirit and it's not lovely; it's gluttonous. It's perverse, no matter how you want to argue it and there are lots of arguments out there. I've heard them many times over, and so have you: that a woman shouldn't be judged by what she wears; it's her body and her business. But if we are claiming Christ, it isn't our body; it's His. And as His body, it's His business how we are bearing His image to the world (1 Corinthians 6:15-17). I urge us to consider this, because women who desire to love well aren't interested in empty flattery, anyway. They aren't interested in using provocative means by which to gain attention to themselves because they live in recognition that a holy God lives inside of them and His glory should be shining from within them.

Maturity and godliness protect the purity that is ours through marriage, so our obedience in the matter of modesty benefits our sexuality. In spite of what the world is telling you about feminism, God's voice should be louder. It's His celebration that our hearts should be after, not society's, because what they desire is in direct opposition to the ways and will of God (James 4:4). They say it's your right, but He says your body is His temple (1 Corinthians 6:19). They say we're free to be sexual, but He says it's shameful outside of marriage (Romans 13:14). This doesn't mean that once you're married you can bear it all. What God desires are that we bear His name to all people for His glory and bear all our curves for the sweet seduction and exclusive invitation within our marital encounters.

I want you to believe the value that Christ has placed on you and the call He has given you to bear His beauty in your life. You don't have to show your body or your booty to prove you are confident. According to scripture, you're worth more than that!

"Your beauty should not come from outward adornment, such as elaborate hairstyles and the wearing of gold jewelry or fine clothes. Rather, it should be that of your inner self, the unfading beauty of a gentle and quiet spirit, which is of great worth in God's sight." - 1 Peter 3:3-4 (ESV)

When we honor our bodies, we honor the Lord. When we honor our husbands, we honor the Lord. A marriage relationship should be the only source for sensual complements and sexual approval and the only one who should have an invitation into your sexuality should be your husband. Orgasmic-like expressions posted in social Apps won't honor anyone. 100 likes from strangers, and then what? A lustful look from someone else won't move your husband's heart and it won't reflect the glory of God in your life. We all pray for "Boaz" but are we living lives like "Ruth"? It's something to consider because our choices produce results.

Listen, if in my marriage, I am still seeking ways to gain sexual attraction from members outside of my marriage, I am operating outside of purity. The standards to keep clean hands and pure hearts don't expire after marriage. We can have sex, be sexy, express our sexuality and entice our husbands and still be pure when these advances and exchanges are done within our marriages. But if our bodies are being used as tools to gain outside attention rather than as a gift to offer within our intimate moments in marriage, we are not honoring God, we are not honoring our husbands and we are not honoring ourselves (1 Corinthians 6:18).

What we share gets seen and maybe even sometimes saved. What you wear in public gets noticed by someone and, as women who desire to love well, we need to consider others more than ourselves (Mark 12:31). Though we've been conditioned to believe that our rights or "our truth" should be elevated above other opinions, this is not what scripture teaches at all. If what I'm doing causes someone else to fall, it becomes wrong even if it is my right to do it. Though I have the right to wear whatever I'd like, if it is a distraction to other women's husbands or to my brothers in Christ, it's wrong.

"… count others more significant than yourselves. Let each of you look not only to his own concerns, but also to the concerns of others."
– Philippians 2: 3-4 (ASV)

Our rights do not take precedence over God's Word. If we desire to be women who love well, we've got to think of other people, other women and other Believers. We should be considering how our dress will reflect on our husbands, how our outfit may or may not honor the wife of another man, how our clothes could affect onlookers from the opposite sex and ultimately, how our attire will be pleasing to the Lord. Just because you can't control if someone lusts after you doesn't mean you aren't responsible for creating an opportunity for them to do so. We are our brother's keepers and if we desire to be women who love well, that means we have to love our neighbors and consider how our actions and choices will affect other people's thoughts, personal lives, struggles and perspectives.

What's been discussed may not be of much concern to you, but if you do sense the Lord addressing you, I want you to know you're not alone. I want you to know that you're not a failure; you're growing and you're becoming and it's a process. I have gone through many seasons of discarding skirts and plunging necklines from my own closet. I've had to sew on extra fabric onto favorite dresses. I've had to delete pictures posted 10 years ago. The Holy Spirit brings correction to our attention to protect us, and it becomes a blessing when we obey!

I'd like to encourage each of us to take some inventory and allow the Holy Spirit to speak to our hearts concerning our bodies, our modesty and our marriages. Once we focus on God's presence in our union, our concern won't be about how we look to others anymore, instead, we'll have an assurance that our marital sexuality is satisfied, and God is glorified! In turn, the excitement of our exclusivity can ignite greater passion wherever and however we choose! Once we stop seeking our advice and affirmations from a corrupt world that is fading away, our desires to be desired will fall completely in the hands of our husbands, whose love isn't limited to empty flattery or lustful limitations.

Sex Talk Not Trash Talk

Now that we have confidence that God is pleased with our marital sex, we should start owning it and grow in it and be more aware of what our husbands need and what we desire. However, studies have shown that many marriages struggle in doing just that – surveying our interests and expectancies when it comes to sex.

An article by Psychology Today revealed that embarrassment is the number one problem recorded in online relationship forums. Three out of five couples, particularly wives, admit to feeling awkward and embarrassed to discuss their sexual, preferences, needs or curiosities with their spouse.[22] This surprised me to read and I feel it's a hindrance that needs to be push out of the way and out of our lives because a thriving marriage shouldn't embody embarrassment in our sexual exploits. Since we have been given freedom and permission by God to explore our marital sexuality, we shouldn't be hindering our drives by refusing to discuss what we like or enjoy. There is no doubt in my mind that we're all willing to become more loving in our marriages, but love making is part of that, too! Being a good lover means walking in your God given confidence to enjoy sex, unashamedly, because sex is God's gift to you both. In marriage,

---

[22] Gratzo, Allen. *Sexual Communication in the Modern Era.* Anchor Book Press, 2007.

it's pure, it's lovely and it's a command; not a suggestion, a command (Genesis 1:28).

"Many women tend to take the wrong course of action, feeling insecure about developing sexually ... most tend to feel there are a lot of "supposed to" 's, as if they are supposed to perform this way or feel that way in a sexual encounter. But good lovers talk about their feelings and they talk about sex." [23] Don't you just love that? Good lovers talk about love making! And don't we all want to be a good lover? It's allowed in your marriage, you know? It's ok. You can say it out loud, "I want to be a good lover!" Refusing the openness to discuss anything is a reflection of insecurity, but your marriage should be a safe place to explore all matters pertaining to your love and devotion to one another.

So how do we become better lovers and take the uncertainties out of our intimate moments and discussions with our husbands? We do this the same way we become better friends, better mothers and better wives ... we talk and we listen. We have pillow talk, send sext messages, read books, ask questions, explore answers, share ideas and create new ones. We must be willing to venture out and uncover our undisclosed thoughts for the enhancement of our intimate encounters with one another. Though we all want our husbands to be in tuned with us, it's our responsibility to teach him

---

[23] Karson, M. *Six Common Problems Couples Have with Sex*. Routledge, 2014.

what we desire and learn what he enjoys. Your husband might be able to guess what you like (or don't like), but he can't be sure unless you tell him. So, talking about what you want, sexually, is a good thing and it's allowed. It's not icky or weird or wrong. It's not trashy; It's fun and it's important because you both are changing and will continue to do so. Communication and exploration help you learn together so that neither of you misses each other's steps.

As a young child, I made the commitment to maintain virginity until marriage. I certainly endured my own set of temptations and struggles, but by the grace of God, the Lord's faithfulness made this goal possible. Though marriage opened the door to freedoms in my sexuality, there were a few things to work out in our early married season. Uncertain and unfamiliar, I was very hesitant in discussing my beginning sexual experiences with Jarrett in our new lives together. Eventually, I mustered up the courage to share my feelings and thoughts of nervousness. I confessed that I had been too embarrassed to say something to him because I didn't want him to see me as immature and I didn't want him to become hesitant towards me in our marital moments together. His response was very tender and reassuring and the conversations that followed taught me so much about my own body and about his body, his preferences and my pleasure. Jarrett's gentle assurances made all the difference for my feelings, concerns and thoughts. After also talking to my doctor and gaining further insights, things got figured out rather quickly! A couple of beaches, lake boats, two babies and seven years later, those early anxieties I had seem like trifle little hiccups now!

The point of this story is that I opened up and talked with my husband about what I was feeling, what I was thinking, expecting and wanting. I had to point and show and let him touch and do whatever was necessary so that he could learn my body and so I could learn his. Friendly exploration such as this can truly enhance sexual experiences. We can't just hope it'll all work out. If we never discuss it, there's no guarantee that either one of you will discover what is unknown or unseen. I realize some of you might be shy to read this; others of you are lapping this up! But it's something we all think about in the corners of our minds, because we want great marriages and we want great sex! No need to be shy about it and no need to be ashamed of it.

Practically every movie or TV show slips in some degree of sexual exchanges between people who are not married or between two people who may be married to other people. It's ungodly, but common, however their misuse shouldn't give you shame. Own your freedom and enjoy your man! You are free, through Christ's love over your marriage and over your lives.

God designed your body, your marriage and your preferences. If you are struggling in your current marriage due to a misuse of sex in your past, please hold tight to the truth that there is no condemnation for those who are in Christ Jesus (Romans 8:1). Whatever you saw or did or said or felt or whatever was done to you way back when doesn't have to be a part of your marriage. You are dearly loved, and you are totally free! Please stop feeling awkward about your sexuality with your husband and talk with him about what you want and how you feel. As you and your husband grow closer to each other through time and seasons, here are some questions you can explore together to have a better understanding of how you can better meet one another's needs:

1) Are there any uncertainties or concerns I'm harboring about sex that I need to discuss with my husband so that we both feel loved, satisfied and secure?

2) How can I initiate doing something different and new to romance my husband, in and out of the bedroom?

3) I may not prefer doing …, but would doing so be harmful or helpful for my husband and his needs?

Asking questions such as these and then sharing your heart with your husband doesn't have to be a scary thing. He is your husband. He loves you; you love him, and you are in covenant, together. You both desire to please and honor each other and the Lord. This is a good thing, so you can let your guard down, be spontaneous, initiate sex to mix things up and explore one another in whatever ways you'd like! Sometimes, it takes a conversation to get you started! You can talk before and after you have sex, or even during your lovemaking, if you're comfortable with that. It's not so much about when you talk, it's more important that you do talk in order to discover new things about each other! You can start sharing your feelings and your daydreams about your evenings together. Wake him up early in the morning before the kids get up! Put something lacey in his pocket on his way out the door to work. Tell him what you like. Husbands like that kind of stuff! You might find it awkward or embarrassing at first, but be brave! There should be no hindrances in your marriage and talking about what you're already thinking about is healthy and it's enjoyable! Sex becomes a lot better when you each are more knowledgeable about what pleases the other, so don't hold back! Give it all you've got, relax and enjoy!

<u>Declining with Grace</u>

We know, by natural composition, most men can just go and go! Some women have surges of immense sexual appetites and stamina, as well, but there are days when this just isn't going to be the case. We have to be careful, in moments such as these, to not allow sex to turn into a duty or chore; rather focus on the enjoyment, instead, and be gracious to one another if the time just isn't right. Sex should never be a burden and it should never be done robotically. It takes patience, love and care and we know it takes some TLC to romance a woman properly. Some women need more time and efforts than others to become aroused and ready to go, but sometimes, we just don't want to go anywhere at all.

Taking a walk with a friend of mine, we discussed the process of declining. She felt so drained because, like clockwork, her husband would come home from work each day and immediately take her upstairs. Sometimes, there wasn't even a conversation beforehand. She told me it used to be so thrilling at first but over time, it became a dread, because she felt like there was no romance involved. There were other more spontaneous moments she did enjoy, but the "Honey, I'm home" routine made her want to dig a hole in the ground and hide away! After months of this, she finally had a heart to heart with her husband and shared that she felt rushed and pushed and that she preferred more foreplay, more conversation and less frequency. With teary eyes, she expressed her needs for him to slow it down and create an environment for more romance so that she could feel like a wife and not a stress-reliever. Her husband was very moved, quick to apologize and confided that he had no idea it was so upsetting because all he could do on his commute from work was think about her and couldn't wait to get home to sweep her off her feet.

It's very possible, in cases such as these, where spouses long to please the other but wires can get crossed and intentions can get misunderstood. At no point in marriage should either one of you go through the motions of sex as if it is your duty. That's not loving or giving, it's obligation and it won't produce mutual love or respect in marriage. It's ok to say "no", sometimes; but it's imperative on how we say it because men love to have sex with their wives. They are wired differently than we are, so we have to be sure to explain to them ways in which sex can be more mutually fulfilling. At times, these conversations may need to be addressed on a day to day basis, depending on how someone might be feeling. We could wake up sexual but go to be uninterested. We could be hormonal from our cycles or too emotional with thoughts and feelings pertaining to other matters. Work could be stressful, the kids could be impossible and sometimes, it's just not a good time for sex. It happens. But we should be considerate enough of our husband's feelings to explain our feelings in truthful and loving ways.

We've all seen the common "headache" excuses on TV and jokes that some disinterested women use to avoid sex, but making up reasons is dishonest and immature. We need to communicate how we're feeling so that avoidance doesn't turn into drawn out seasons of sexual rejection which could be very wounding and discouraging in a marriage.

"Do not deprive one another, except by mutual consent and for a time, so you may devote yourselves to prayer. Then come together again, so that Satan will not tempt you through your lack of self-control…"
— 1 Corinthians 7:5 (NIV)

If you don't want to, you don't want to. There's no need to lie or avoid your husband as if a disinterest is the problem, because it's not. Unwillingness is the danger, because unwillingness is a form of refusal and refusal is rejection. We need to learn how to decline with grace and assure our husbands that we do desire them and enjoy being pleasured by them. Instead of shaming them for desiring us, we must learn to assure them in loving ways while still operating in honesty, because a wife who wants to love well is sensitive to her husband's sexual drive, which the Lord gave him. This doesn't mean that husbands shouldn't be sensitive to their wife's bodies, feelings and sexual preferences, because they most very well should, however, in this book, we are looking at marital sex from a wife's viewpoint.

There is no doubt that you do, in fact, desire to love well, but there is nothing wrong with declining for the right reasons. It's so important to not reject out of spite or punishment. This is very unloving and not behooving of a woman of noble character. Studies have shown that men who experience repetitive sexual rejection can begin to internalize low self-esteem, indifference and depression.[24] This takes a toll on a marriage in various ways. Though they seem strong, men can be vulnerable, too. Rejections without reason (real reason) can develop doubt and worry, so it is very unhealthy in marriage for one spouse to continually decline the other out of rejection or indifference. This is why the Bible tells us not to deprive one another, "except by mutual consent" – mutual meaning that both are aware of the other's feelings and thus can properly navigate best choices, together.

There are so many factors as to why one might need to decline an evening of passion. Many of us work hard outside of the home, tend to children and house affairs in addition to our personal lives, church involvement, families, businesses and so on. Some of us are pregnant and don't want to. Some of us just had babies and are simply too tired and unavailable. Some of us need time and space to process arguments before we can strip down and roll around, and

---

[24] Kimmel, M. S. (2005). The Gender of Desire: Essays on Male Sexuality. Albany, NY: State University of New York Press.

that's understandable. The point is that, at some point, we need to be gracious and give ourselves into our marriages. We know sex is a beautiful opportunity to connect to each other in ways beyond the mere physical, so even when we're not feeling it, it's important that we consider each other's needs first. This may not look like three times a day, seven days a week, but the two of you can learn to consider one another and do what's best in order to flourish.

I personally have learned to use, "not now", as opposed to "no", because the latter is final whereas the former leads to availability for another time. It's important to me, as Jarrett's wife, that he knows I am always willing, but sometimes unable, so I am very careful in the times where I choose to decline by reassuring him that we'll get to it at another time in the very near future. It's important, to me, that he knows I desire him, so the times when I do decline, I will reach for him and initiate once I am ready. This is my way to be gracious and reassuring. We must all develop our own manner because it's a part of life and a part of marriage. Not every time will be the right time, but I urge you to use loving ways to address the matter. Don't make fun or breathe loudly or roll eyes or turn over. Tell him how you're feeling. Your husband truly wants to please you and be pleased by you. Cut him some slack and if you have to decline, do it with grace and dignity. Kiss him lightly and reassure him of your love and your desire to intertwine later. If we are to be women who love well, we've got to be sure that all our responses are loving and gracious, even our declines.

Kids in the Mix

Now we know love making makes lovely babies. If you weren't aware, that is end result! Sex is for mutual pleasure and that pleasure produces an inheritance (Psalm 127:3). The Bible says our children are like arrows in our lives, forging the future while our wisdom and love trail behind them. Kids are wonderful and lovely and messy and loud! They are our joy; they are also our distraction so, it is imperative that we do not fall prey to the temptation of centering our lives around them.

One of the most common mistakes couples can make is to center their marriage around their children.[25] It's easy for us, as mothers, to transfer our affection, time and attention primarily on our babies, but in our efforts to be good mothers, we cannot overlook our husbands and expect our marriages to continue to thrive. A woman who desires to love well will not only include her husband but entrust him to be a father while also making time for him away from the children so that marriage remains in its proper place. Remember, your marriage is about you and him, not you and them. Children need to see their parents loving on each and devoted to one another, apart from them. This brings stability, confidence, securityand identity to their lives. They need to see you modeling a marriage relationship with the exchanges of godly love, respect and

---

[25] Mascolo, Michael F., *Eight Keys to Old School Parenting for Modern-Day Families*, Nelson Press, 2015.

commitment. This requires that we as parents take time away from our children to focus on our marriage and reignite some passion that our children can see in the home.

Ladies, your children will teach you about the covering of Christ – a lesson your husband would have had a head start in learning through the Lord's commission he's given him over you. There is nothing like marriage to teach a man the unconditional love of Jesus and there is nothing like raising children that will teach a woman the same. It's a common misconception that a family begins when the children arrive, but the truth is that your marriage made you and your husband a family before the babies ever came and it's this relationship that created your children, so keeping a strong connection between the two of will be important in the continual development of a healthy and thriving family. A family is produced through marriage and a marriage involves sex. We have to be intentional and deliberate in protecting our sex lives and our marriage relationship from stagnancy in our efforts to raise our children. Give yourself permission to prioritize this relationship in the midst of creating relationships with your children. Finding the time and energy to love your husband, away from the kids, will propel your love for one another so that when you are with your kids, that love continues to permeate in their presence.

Our eldest daughter was two weeks old when Jarrett and I had our first date, post-baby. Not everyone may feel comfortable with this, but she was with my mother and I do believe that relying on people you can trust makes a big difference when it comes to carving out time for consistent date nights. This is so pivotal in maintaining a thriving sex life, even after the kids, because the measure in which we are connecting outside of the home can affect the quality of connecting lovingly inside of the home. Your kids need to you loving each other; therefore, you need to be sure to invest in loving each other apart from them.

Life for us is busy and overflowing, now that we are a family of four, but we make time in our week for moments meant for just the two of us and we keep our date nights consistent. I calendar our outings and set reservations in advanced, because time away is a priority that should be planned. Relying on spontaneity in dating your spouse can be difficult once children come along, so don't assume that something planned can't be exciting. We calendar meetings, vacations, workout schedules and other events of importance, don't we? Therefore, there is nothing wrong with doing the exact same thing with your love life. People make time for what's important to them and it's essential to make time for your marriage so that you don't lose touch with one another in pursuit of pouring into your kids. Be creative and be intentional.

3:00 am. That's my time. I sometimes write, I sometimes do laundry, I often wake up Jarrett. This may seem like an inconvenience for some people, but for us, it's an ideal opportunity. See, once the girls are tucked in bed, most of our evenings are spent in exhaustion over a cup of decaf coffee and a movie, reading a book together or sitting around our fire pit. For us, 9pm is slow down time. But 3am? That's the right time, for us! Of course, I'm japing with my words. It's not a hard core 3am with timers and bells. What I mean is, sometimes, you have to be just as creative about when you have sex as much as how you have sex. Making love isn't about absolutes. Date nights aren't always about spending money. Location, time of day, position … those things change, and kids make it change, so being flexible is very important! Don't limit yourself with "supposed to" 's. Great sex can take place at 8am just as well as 8pm and when kids show up, we all soon find out what an interruption parenting can be on our intimacy. Afternoon sex won't exist anymore when Elmo comes on at lunch time. And don't get me started on when the kids get old enough to jump in bed with you in the middle of the night. I have no idea when that started, but I think, for now, it's an expected occurrence in our home.

Once our sweet children arrive, virtually every sense of our routines will change. These children we prayed for bless our lives in ways unimaginable, but they also come with their own set of modifications that we don't always account for. Intimacy is one of those changes and sometimes it can cause us to mourn the days of long ago. "Me" time fades, date night becomes more complicated and sex can sometimes suffer, as well. The new responsibility of parenting can really take a toll and many women struggle to balance being good mothers and being good wives.

Listen, you're going to mess up. It's ok. You're not failing, you're learning and you're doing a good job! I'm cheering you on, but I am also challenging you to remember who you were before your kids came into the world. Don't lose sight of yourself and don't lose sight of your husband, either. As the mother, it's so normal to turn into full on nurturing mode, but cutting out the sexual side of who you are is not healthy. You are still a wife, you are still a woman and your husband needs to know that he is still your number one. Your children also need to know that your husband is number one, as this will instill healthy boundaries in your home, in your parenting and in the identity of your children.

According to Psychology Today, "Child-centered parenting runs the risk of producing entitled, narcissistic children, who lack the capacity to persevere and cope with responsibility and community. This is because there is a fine line between being "loving" and being "indulgent". Indulgent children are spoiled children and spoiled things begin to smell. "Indulging our kids is not conducive to preparing individuals who are capable to contribute to the broader society outside of the home".[26] Loving well results in loving others and showing considerate for others. We can teach our children these values by raising them to be a part of our marriages, not the replacement of our marriages. It's important that both you and your husband model for your kids that you are loving, considering and investing in one another. I know the tears are hard to take and I know we worry that our mother's might use old-school tactics, or our aunts might feed them fructose, but a weekend or a few hours away is healthy for our kids and for our marriages.

---

[26] *The Failure of Child-Centered Parenting | Psychology Today.*
www.psychologytoday.com/us/blog/old-school-parenting-modern-day-families/201505/the-failure-child-centered-parenting.

Remember, we are raising our children to be lights in this world, and this means that one day, inevitably, they are going to leave our homes and sojourn on into the world on their own, without us – making their own lives and their own families. In light of this reality, it's so important that we do not sacrifice the health of our marriages in our efforts to raise our children, because once they leave, we are still married to our spouses. Many marriages experience crisis in the empty nest seasons of life because they feel like strangers as a result of putting their parenting first. My father, who counsels countless married couples every year, often expresses the sorrow he feels for families who have centered their marriages and their lives around their children. "Children are going to leave", he reminds Jarrett and I. "Pray for them, raise them, discipline them and love them enough to entrust them to the Lord. That's your calling as parents and while you're doing it, don't forget about each other. If you fall apart, they fall apart."

Ladies, our beautiful marriages need to be priority. There is no human relationship that should put a stint in your marriage. You made vows to your husband, not your children. This may sound harsh, but it's the truth and it needs our attention. Our sweet boys and girls will benefit from a strong, prioritized marriage, but, according to Dr. Gary Thompson, "marriages will suffer if the priority transfers to the kids. This, unfortunately, could cause lasting psychological damage to our children, ironically".[27]

---

[27] Thomas, Gary. *Sacred Parenting: How Raising Children Shapes Our Souls.* Zondervan, 2017.

If our marriage breakdowns, our children will suffer, and the results could be irreversible. I know life makes us tired, and I know you're trying so hard. It feels so exhausting and draining and sometimes, all we can do is hold hands, close our eyes and drift off. There will be days like this, but I'm urging us to stop sleeping on our husbands. I urge us all to stop serving our men our leftover time and excuses. The quality of time invested in your marriage before the kids is still required after the kids. As any new parent understands, babies can bring stress and children contribute to the "working" part of marriage. They demand your attention, all the time, every time, but you are still a sexual being who has pledged your life to another sexual being and he needs you in every way he needed you before your children arrived. Don't put him on the back burner in efforts to cater to his children. Include him, encourage him and keep love making available to him. This benefits you, too!

I'll be honest, some days, the potty training gets the best of me and I get anxious for bedtime so that I can have some "married time". Even if it's just cuddling up to Jarrett while looking through our younger years together, or daydreaming about future vacations or moving into more physical displays of affection, it's all wonderful and very needed! Date night doesn't have to include wild crazy sex, but it's ok if that's what comes of it! Keeping your marriage a priority amidst your mothering will help you stay connected with your husband as a lover and a friend and not just your co-partner. He's more than that and you're more than that. Begin to make time toshow him this if you desire to love him well. Be purposeful. Include him, reach for him, touch him and celebrate him. Intentionality has a dynamic way of maintaining the sparks that created the children in the first place! If reading this has caused you to reflect, I'm cheering you on to re-establish your priorities and then protect them. Your kids are important. Cleaning the house and ascertaining your career are important things. But important things, unprioritized, can become dangerous distractions. Remember, God created marriage to reflect His covenant with us, so marriage only works when it come first before all other human relationships. This isn't always easy, but you were not called to be an easy woman. You were called to be a woman who loves well! In so doing, your love will draw your husband and your children closer to you and you can help draw them closer to Christ.

Encouragement Just for You

Loving God's way will result in becoming a woman who loves well. The Lord is pleased and honored when our marriages reflect His love, as He designed for it to be. In this way, we can focus our attention on cultivating our internal beauty of love, respect, grace, forgiveness and humble hearts within our homes as well as with the world around us. As we grow in our pursuit of the eternal and unconditional love of God through Jesus, our blooming spiritual awareness will begin to re-shape our marriages, our sexuality and even how we see ourselves and how we love our husbands and others. My friends, it's been seven years for me, and I've not done it all right, but who among us is perfect? I know I sure am not, but our God is and He provides us with all the love we need in Christ! His love is perfect and compels us to pursue loving well in all our relationships, but first and foremost, our marriages.

I can honestly tell you that my marriage does not have a secret sauce. It has the love of Christ. Every day, I see Jesus practiced in my home, through the way my husband loves me and through the way I love him. This affirms our marriage and protects our children. It's this love that compels me to respond in loving ways to my husband, my family and the world. It has made all the difference in my life and it has motivated me to go deeper in Christ so that I can have the spiritual wisdom to know how to love my husband in flourishing ways. That's the point of marriage: to show us that our love is not enough. We need something more to sustain us and propel us past feelings and conditions and into faith and unconditional love. It's Jesus. It's His love that transforms our hearts to love well in all seasons and in every situation. It's possible and it's imperative and it's available to anyone who desires to receive it! No matter where you are in your marriage, God has a plan for you. We're all flawed, but our short comings do not define our marriages. Our love defines our marriages and God's love determines the degrees in which we choose to love.

My ending notes of encouragement for each of us is this: desire to be a woman who loves well, not because of the benefits, but because it points to Jesus. Loving well requires that we put all distractions to the side so that we can focus on what matters most:

each other. It's not always easy, but … you guessed it … we were never called to be easy women. We have been called to be valiant women, seated high in heavenly places, authorized to speak life in every situation, command victory even in the midst of our trials and to serve our families with humility and grace, just as Christ does for each of us. Allowing the Holy Spirit room in our hearts to implement these virtues will produce a godly marriage. This is the proof of a Christ filled heart. It's what propels us to love well and positions us to be loved well. Jesus makes all the difference. So, let His love inside and watch how it directs your steps to love deeper and fuller, beyond the vows and beyond the "now". We're looking into eternity ladies. Loving well will take us there!

Reflection

Which section in this chapter meant the most to you and why? How can you apply this to your life and to your marriage?

<u>Scriptures for Your Soul</u>

"Let him kiss me with the kisses of his mouth — for your love is more delightful than wine."
-Song of Solomon 1:2

"For you have been bought with a price: therefore, glorify God in your body."
-1 Corinthians 6:20

PRAYERS FOR EVERY SEASON

<u>Prayers for Us All</u>

There is no way I could cover every single aspect of loving well, but I know that the love of Christ sees us all exactly where we are and exactly where we are meant to be. In my seven years of love, I have learned much, but I know I still have much to learn. My prayer for us all is that, in our pursuits of loving well, we will allow the perfect love of Jesus to draw us closer to Him so that we can be the women He is calling us to be.

We are all in process and progress, so our hope must be set on what Jesus will accomplish in us, rather than what we can endeavor to do on our own. I urge you to take truthful inventory of how you are loving your husband, how you are loving others and how you are loving the Lord. How we treat people matters and it will reflect what is in our inner hearts, more so than our words ever will. If you desire to truly love well, I encourage you to begin by trusting God's heart for you. His love sets all other love into motion!

Know that I am cheering you on every step of the way and that your desire to keep Christ at the center will result in many blessings for your current moment and every season yet to come!

To the Wife Who Is Waiting

"Wives, in the same way submit yourselves to your own husbands so that, if any
of them do not believe the word, they may be won over without words by the
behavior of their wives, when they see the purity and reverence of your lives."
- 1 Peter 3:1-2 (NIV)

Dear Lord,

I pray over every husband who does not yet know you. I pray along side every sweet wife who feels alone in her spiritual journey, who attends church by herself, who endures sarcasm about her faith or who is simply ignored and overlooked. Lord, I pray that your spirit will comfort and protect, cover and lead. Use your sweet daughters to express your unconditional love and be faithful to your Word that declares that her love for you will draw her husband to you. I thank you for the future salvation that will take place in homes all around this world because of faithful wives who desire to love well. I pray salvation over children and that your Holy Spirit will guide families into your love and into your truth. Family is your divine design and we know that you are doing a work, even though we can't always see it. Thank you, Lord, for every heart that cries out to you on behalf of the salvation of their husband and their families.

In Jesus' holy name,

Amen

<u>To the Wife Who Longs for a Child</u>

"For the Lord God is our sun and our shield. He gives us grace and glory. The Lord will withhold no good thing from those who do what is right."

-Psalm 84:11

Dear Jesus,

There are so many hurting hearts, begging for children and begging for a blessing. Please reassure them that they are already blessed. Your Word promises that you will not withhold any good thing from your children. Comfort my sisters and give them grace and mercy, just as you did for Hannah, as she cried out to you for pregnancy (1 Samuel 1:11).

Lord, we know that you know all things and that your plans for us are good and promised and purposed. Help us to Trust that you truly are working out miracles and teach your daughters to rest in your love and to rely on the love of the husbands you've blessed them with. May their faith grow ever stronger in you and may you become their Prince of peace as they sojourn through this difficult season. You promised to never leave us or forsake us, so I thank you Lord that you are always near.

In Jesus' name,

Amen.

To the Wife Who Has Lost Her Title

"The Lord is near to the brokenhearted and saves the crushed in spirit."

-Psalm 34:18

Lord Jesus,

I want to lift up every tear and every despair that may be felt in the hearts of my sisters. Divorce is devastating and I know some precious ladies may be struggling in the process or consideration of divorce. It's difficult and terrifying, but even in the flames, in the storms, and the valleys, you've promised to be there. Please be their banner. Wipe every tear from their eye. Replace their fear with faith, their anger with worship, their anxiety with your peace and their uncertainty with a deeper trust in you. Teach them how to choose forgiveness and give them the strength to let go of any resentment that desires to erode away their relationship with you. Protect children that could be affected by this process and guard their hearts as they depend deeper on you in this trying season.

Thank you, Lord, that divorce is not the end, and should there be opportunities for reconciliation, I ask that your Holy Spirit soften hearts and restore homes.

We praise you in our trials and we trust you with the outcomes.

In Christ's name we pray,

Amen.

<u>To the Wife Who Feels Betrayed</u>

"The steadfast love of the Lord never ceases; his mercies never come to an end"

-Lamentations 3:22

Faithful Lord,

Nothing shakes you and nothing deters you. Your love is steadfast and never changing. I pray my sisters hold tight to the love that your sacrifice has poured out over them. I pray that they hold tight to the hope that your salvation brings. Anchor their hearts in your unconditional love as they look to you for answers and comfort and peace. Unfaithfulness of any kind is shattering. We marry in full confidence but an affair or a lack of love in our marriage alters the trust and security that once existed in a marriage. God, be an anchor for our souls. Though trust is never easily restored, there is hope in in you, Lord! We know that your love can heal all our wounds and all our scars. Lord let us love like you. Even in our pain, teach us to love like you and to shine our light in dark seasons, because you see us and you care.

For every woman suffering with a broken heart due to unfaithfulness, I pray over their lives and I ask that you will be their strength.

In Jesus' mighty name I pray,

Amen.

To the Single Woman Longing to Become a Wife

"Pursue love, and earnestly desire the spiritual gifts"
-1 Corinthians 14:1

Father in Heaven,

There is little that stings our hearts as deeply as desiring to find a love all our own. So, Lord, I pray for every woman who's heart desires marriage. I pray Lord that their prayers for romantic love won't distract them from their daily mission to love like you. Condition their hearts to remember that your gifts are spiritual and lead them into mission that will provide them an outlet to give and receive and grow in your love, as you direct their steps and guide their paths. Though singleness can be very discouraging, it has a purpose. One of the worst things often said to single sisters is that their loneliness is a blessing. I know it doesn't feel like a blessing, so I pray you will guide them into authentic pursuits to living and loving well, for You! Chase their hearts to invest their time in relationship with You, Lord, rather than petitioning for romance. Your love is the greatest and will equip them to love greatly whomever you choose to enter into their lives. Help us all to trust your timing and your process and give each sweet sister faith to wait for your promises to unfold in their lives.

In Your precious and holy name,

Amen

A Prayer You Can Pray

Dear Lord,

I thank you for your blessing of marriage. Let your love radiate in my family. God, I pray over my husband! I call out his name and I lift up his heart to you. Bless all of his endeavors and protect him as he creates opportunities for our family. Please give me a gentle heart, full of grace and compassion and understanding for his leadership. Give me the strength and wisdom to champion him on in his efforts to do good, to respect his decisions while still pushing him for greater. Teach me how to motivate him and inspire him to become all that you are preparing and equipping him for. Teach me how to love him unconditionally and how to support his dreams and uplift his efforts. Help me love him well, Lord. Lead me to love him the way you love me. Whatever our marriage is going through or will go through, my eyes are fixed on you and I trust your plans for my household. I trust your plans of salvation for my family and I trust your beautiful plans for my life, my love and my role as Mrs.____.

I give all my anxious thoughts to you, Lord. I give all of my regrets, mistakes, fears, joys, anticipation and future to you, God. Teach me to love well. My marriage is your tool. My life is your treasure and I trust you to complete the good work you started in me and in my marriage.

It's in Jesus' name I pray,

Amen

Questions & Answers with
Jarret and Katrina

These questions were collected from Katrina's Instagram. You can follow her there @_katrinakatrina_

Q: What attracted you to each other?

Katrina: He was very honest and intense. I often dated flashy guys who bragged a lot, but I found Jarrett's quiet confidence to be more attractive.

Jarrett: I saw her right-away. She was tall and beautiful and always helping others. She also has this really sweet voice and she laughs really, really loud! I just thought she was unlike anyone I'd ever known. She was a challenge, though, and I liked that, too!

Q: What's it like to be married?

Jarrett: Like sports. Sometimes you cheer and score points and then there are times when you feel like you're sitting on the bench. But I have to say that I love being a husband and having someone who cares about my feelings all the time.

Katrina: Marriage is lovely! There's no other way to put it. It's difficult though; it's not always glamorous. Our different families and different past experiences cause us to work at creating our own lifestyle, but that's what makes it so wonderful!

Q: Who said, "I love you first"?

Jarrett: KATRINA!

Katrina: I blurted it out like an idiot! But he did say it back, though!

Q: *Have you ever wished you were still single?*

Katrina: Nope. I love being married and I love my husband. We are really blessed in our marriage and we really enjoy loving each other!

Jarrett: Ever since I met Katrina, all I wanted was to be married to her and that has never changed.

Q: *Jarrett, when did you know you wanted to put a ring on it?*

Jarrett: Our second date! But we dated two years and two months before I was in a place where I knew I was prepared and mature enough to ask her to marry me… well, to ask her Dad!

Q: *What has been the best and worst part of your marriage?*

Jarrett: The worst part of our marriage is also the best part. It was the day our daughter was born. Katrina almost died, but God is good and He protected her. It was a crazy night, but it was definitely one of the first miracles in our marriage.

Katrina: The best part of our marriage, for me, has been seeing Jarrett grow into a father. He's very loving, kind and strong. I think he's had a lot of practice with my personality! The worst part of our marriage, for me, has been in-law conflicts. I'm learning to love well through it.

Q: *Was it hard abstaining from pre-marital sex?*

Jarrett: Yes! I wasn't sure if I could do it, but I'm really glad we waited. I know it was my relationship with Christ that helped me.

Katrina: It wasn't hard in our dating, but it became a new struggle in our engagement, which really disappointed me about myself. Jarrett was very mature to hold us accountable and help me focus on my desire to remain a virgin until marriage. God guided us for sure! It was definitely worth it!

Q: What is your perfect date night?

Katrina: Anything that requires me to put on heels and be out of the house! We really enjoy live shows like Jazz bands or the Ballet. Also, anything involving food – dessert, especially!

Jarrett: I like staying in, but I don't mind taking her out. She likes getting dressed up and she's always very pretty and stylish. Every now and then, I sneak in something sports related, but really, I like doing anything with her!

Q: Since you were celibate, how did you know you'd be sexually compatible?

Katrina: Sexual compatibility is simple: if you're open to having sex with each other, then you're sexually compatible. I think we stress ourselves out too much over sex. It's a wonderful experience that our bodies were made for so once you're married, just enjoy!

Jarrett: Compatibility is found in the relationship not in the sex, but the sex will be compatible if the relationship is healthy and loving.

Q: What is some advice you would give to someone who is engaged?

Jarrett: Invest in marital counseling because it forces you to be honest with yourself and with each other, rather than sweeping things under the carpet. I didn't realize how important it would be!

Katrina: I agree! There are so many unknowns that get revealed in counseling. You can't expect to do something well if you aren't willing to invest in it and accept the challenge to mature and grow.

Q: How do you keep your marriage fun?

Jarrett: I flirt with her a lot which embarrasses her, but I know she loves it! Katrina is a very deep person, so being thoughtful and creative makes her happy and keeps things exciting.

Katrina: Spending time and sharing new experiences with each other and intentionally making memories and moving past predictability. Predictability kills passion.

Q: Do you have any marriage mentors?

Jarrett: Yes, we go to Katrina's parents and I really appreciate my relationship with them and I admire their marriage. We go to them for advice and prayer about lots of different things.

Katrina: My Mom and Dad are so transparent and honest and they challenge us to move from feelings and into truth.

Q: How do you keep God in your marriage?

Jarrett: God is in our marriage because God is in our lives. We are both Saved and constantly building our relationship with Jesus and that spills over into our marriage and parenting.

Katrina: We both live to please Jesus as a way of life, every day; not just on Sundays. He's our life and sustainer of our love!

Conversation Starters to Help You Grow

Communication helps us discover one another so that we can better love each other. Make an evening of asking and responding to these questions together so that you can grow in deeper and fuller love!

1. What was the happiest period of our marriage and what were the reasons you think so?

2. What's something I can change in my life that would improve our marriage?

3. Are we equally invested in cultivating a God-centered marriage? Are we being intentional? If yes, how so? If no, what is hindering us?

4. Do I handle conflict in a mutually loving and respectful way? How can I improve?

5. In what ways do I love you well? How can I improve?

6. Is there another married couple we can reach out to for support in how to love well and how to grow stronger in our marriage and in Christ? Are we intentional about connecting with them? Why or why not?

7. What is the biggest mistake made in our marriage? How can we heal to prevent resentment?

8. In what ways has your love matured for me? Be specific.

9. What is your vision and prayer for our marriage and our family? Are you intentionally seeking God for these things?

10. Do you think the Lord is pleased with our marriage? How are we honoring Him in the way we are living and loving each other, our family and our extended loved ones? Do we need to reevaluate our spiritual relationship with God in any way? How can we start today?

To Those Who Love Me Well:

Acknowledgements

After publishing my first book, Beyond Being Good, I never thought I'd have the ability to write a second. The Lord put this book on my heart, giving me the desire and creativity to complete it and I'm so very thankful and pray that it will accomplish whatever it is He desires for it to do.

I'd like to thank my beautiful husband, Jarrett McCain, for pursuing me and making me his wife. This book would not be possible without his love for me. Jarrett, I'm so honored and blessed to be Mrs. McCain and I love you more and more with each passing year! Cheers to us, Babes! Marrying you has been one of the few things I've done right in my life and God gets all the glory for sure!

To my parents, Reggie and Frances Coleman, I could never say, "Thank you", enough! Thank you for exemplifying what a godly marriage is supposed to look like. Thank you for loving each other in a way that shaped my world view and positioned my heart to desire marriage in my own life. Thank you for showing me that love begins with Christ and that His perfect love makes our love possible. Thank you for being such great examples in my life and in my marriage! And thank you for embracing Jarrett and cheering him on to be the glorious husband and father that he is! We love you both so dearly.

To my daughters, Kailyn and Jaelle. May you always know what loving well looks like by the way I love your father and by the way he loves me! Your existence is proof that God has blessed our marriage and we do not take your hearts or your lives lightly. Even now, your father and I are praying over the futures God is beautifully planning out just for you and my hope is that you will understand your Heavenly Father's love for you by the way we cherish and love you!

To my sweet brother and sister-in-law, Benjamin and Andrea Coleman. I love you both dearly and I am so pleased for all the joy and beauty your marriage has brought to our family and to my life. Thank you, Andrea, for not only being my sister, but also being my friend and for loving my brother so well! Thank you, Ben, for being by my side and on my side and thank you for accepting Jarrett into our family and loving him like a brother! You two mean the world to me! Blessings on you and on my sweet nephew!

To Jazzie, Ashley, BeBe, Christina, Kourtney, Brandi, Tina, Elvira, Jess, Maggie and Sara, I'm so thankful to be connected to your families and your motherhood! I'm so honored to share relationship with you and see how God is using you and your families for His Kingdom and His Gospel! Thank you for pouring your heart into my life. Thank you for holding me accountable, loving me when I am wrong, cheering me on when I am right and always extending your friendship to me. Blessings over your marriages and blessings over your children! I love ya'll!

ABOUT THE AUTHOR

Katrina McCain is a mother of two sweet girls and wife to her best friend, Jarrett. She formerly enjoyed a nine-year modeling career and now works for her church in Charlotte, NC. She writes devotionals for the Bible App, blogs on faith weekly on her website, speaks at events for women of all ages and believes that God's design for love and marriage begins with falling in love with Him, first.

She enjoys deep conversations, writing to encourage others, baking, riding horses, coaching aspiring models, and spending time with her family and friends.

Her first book, *Beyond Being Good: Seeking Christ's Perfection for Our Imperfect Hearts*, was written for any woman who longs to live above performance and into authentic faith in Christ.
Seven Years of Love is Katrina's sophomore project and is a celebration of the beautiful mission of marriage, in every season and circumstance.

You can connect with Katrina and explore more of her heart!
Meet her on Instagram: @_katrinakatrina_
Log onto www.KatrinaMcCain.com